Freeze-Drying Mastery For Beginners Cookbook

---◆○◆---

Create Simple and Delicious Recipes, Save Money on Groceries and Enjoy Homemade Meals All Year Round

By: HarvestGuard Publications

Copyright © 2024 by HarvestGuard Publications – All rights reserved.

No portion of this book may be reproduced in any form without written permission from the publisher or author, except as permitted by U.S. copyright law.

This publication is designed to provide accurate and authoritative information in regard to the subject matter covered. It is sold with the understanding that neither the author nor the publisher is engaged in rendering legal, investment, accounting or other professional services. While the publisher and author have used their best efforts in preparing this book, they make no representations or warranties with respect to the accuracy or completeness of the contents of this book and specifically disclaim any implied warranties of merchantability or fitness for a particular purpose. No warranty may be created or extended by sales representatives or written sales materials. The advice and strategies contained herein may not be suitable for your situation. You should consult with a professional when appropriate. Neither the publisher nor the author shall be liable for any loss of profit or any other commercial damages, including but not limited to special, incidental, consequential, personal, or other damages.

Contents

Download Free Batch Log Booklet	VI
Introduction	IX
Where It All Started	
What You Can Expect	
1. Freeze-Drying Basics	1
Equipment	
Knives and Blades: The Cutting Tools You'll Need	
Other Tools You Might Need	
Best Practices for Efficient and Safe Freeze Drying	
Safety Tips for Using Your Freeze Dryer	
Pretreatments	
When is Dry, Dry Enough?	
Storing Dried Foods: A Drying Guide	
Factors Affecting Drying Times	
Storage: How to Safely Store Freeze-Dried Foods	
Rehydration	
Equivalents	
2. Produce You Will Love	15
Freeze-Dried Food Troubleshooting	
Produce You Will Love and How to Prepare Them	
3. For The Vegetarian In You	29
4. Meat Lovers, These Are For You!	41
5. I Sea Food & I Eat It	53
6. Poultry Dishes You Must Make	65
7. Meals in a Jar	77
8. Yummy Snacks	99

9. Desserts to Die For   111

10. Can't Do Without Candy   123

11. Powders and Smoothies   145

Measurements & Conversions   156
Download Freeze Drying For Beginners Book For Free   157
Conclusion   159
Publisher   161

FREE DOWNLOAD

104 COLOR RECIPES FROM THE BOOK

FREE DOWNLOAD

THE ULTIMATE
BATCH LOG BOOKLET

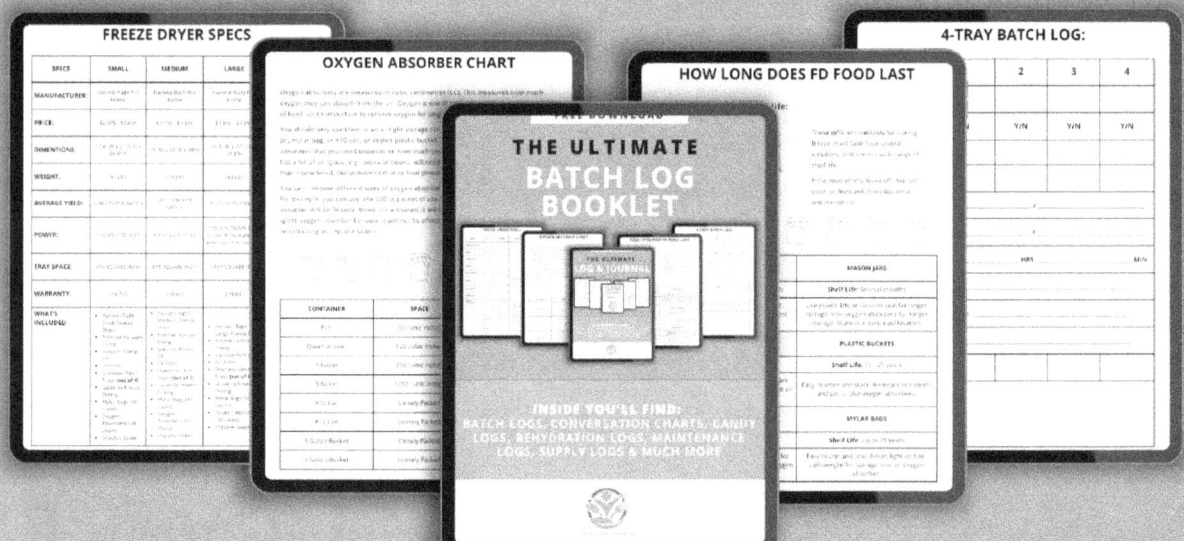

 SCAN ME

Introduction

Welcome to the fascinating world of freeze-drying! In this cookbook, we embark on a culinary journey that transcends conventional cooking methods. We delve into the innovative realm of freeze-drying to unlock a plethora of possibilities in preserving, enhancing flavors, and elevating culinary creations.

Together, we'll explore the ins and outs of freeze-drying, uncovering its secrets, techniques, and myriad applications to revolutionize the way we approach food preservation and preparation.

Where It All Started

As people passionate about outdoor adventures and culinary experimentation, we found ourselves facing the challenge of packing nutritious meals for our backpacking trips without sacrificing taste or adding unnecessary weight to our packs.

As we were preparing for one of these excursions to go deep into the heart of the wilderness, we stumbled upon freeze-dried meals at a local store. Intrigued by the concept, we decided to give it a try. Little did we know that this decision would forever change the way we approached food and outdoor exploration.

From the first bite, we were captivated by the intense flavors and lightweight nature (no pun intended) of freeze-dried meals. Gone were the days of lugging heavy coolers or worrying about perishable ingredients spoiling in the heat. With freeze-dried foods, we could enjoy gourmet meals on the trail without compromising on taste or nutrition.

But our love for freeze-drying didn't end with backpacking trips. Back home, we eagerly experimented with freeze-drying various ingredients, from fruits and vegetables to meats and even candy. We were amazed by the versatility and convenience freeze-drying offered, allowing us to preserve seasonal produce, create innovative recipes, and reduce food waste.

What began as a solution to our outdoor meal dilemmas soon became a passion that permeated every aspect of our lives. Freeze drying became synonymous with adventure, creativity, and a shared love for good food. Whether we were planning our next camping trip or whipping up a gourmet meal in the comfort of our own kitchen, freeze-drying was always at the forefront of our culinary endeavors.

For us, freeze-drying wasn't just a preservation method—it became a lifestyle. It embodied our spirit of exploration, our commitment to sustainability, and our unwavering love for delicious food filled with nutritional value. As we continue to embark on new culinary adventures, freeze-drying remains an integral part of our journey, inspiring us to push the boundaries of flavor, creativity, and outdoor exploration. We hope you'll enjoy this journey with us!

What You Can Expect

While we'll get into the nitty-gritty of freeze-drying in a bit, let's start by unraveling the science behind freeze-drying. Imagine a process where moisture is gently extracted from food, leaving behind its original texture, flavor, and nutritional content intact. Freeze-drying achieves just that by subjecting food to freezing temperatures, followed by a vacuum environment that sublimates the frozen water directly into vapor without passing through the liquid phase. The result? Dehydrated food that retains its essence, rehydrating effortlessly with the addition of water, restoring its original freshness and flavor profile.

Why freeze dry, you ask? There are many benefits, and we mentioned just a few earlier. By preserving food through freeze drying, we extend its shelf life significantly, preserving its nutritional value and flavor for extended periods. Unlike traditional dehydration methods, freeze-drying maintains the food's original texture and appearance, avoiding the shriveling or toughening that often occurs with heat-based drying techniques. Moreover, freeze-dried foods are lightweight, making them ideal for camping, backpacking, emergency preparedness, and space travel. With freeze drying, we unlock a world of culinary possibilities, from gourmet meals to healthy snacks conveniently stored whenever hunger strikes.

We'll also jump into the tools and techniques essential for freeze-drying success. From freeze dryers to trays and containers, we'll explore the equipment needed to embark on our freeze-drying journey. We'll discuss preparation methods, including blanching, slicing, and pre-treating foods to optimize their freeze-drying process. Temperature and timing play crucial roles in freeze drying, and we'll guide you through the intricacies of setting the optimal parameters for different foods, ensuring consistent results every time.

From fruits to proteins, we celebrate the versatility of freeze-dried ingredients. From succulent fruits bursting with flavor to savory meats rich in protein, freeze-drying preserves the essence of each ingredient, offering a bounty of possibilities for culinary experimentation. Whether it's creating vibrant fruit powders for smoothies and desserts or crafting gourmet meals with freeze-dried meats and vegetables, we'll showcase the endless culinary applications of freeze-dried ingredients, inspiring you to unleash your creativity in the kitchen.

Get ready to tantalize your taste buds with our collection of freeze-drying recipes designed to suit every palate and occasion. From vegetarian meal delights and hearty soups in a jar to decadent desserts and savory snacks, we've curated a diverse array of recipes that showcase the versatility and flavor of freeze-dried ingredients. Whether you're a seasoned chef or a culinary novice, our step-by-step instructions and expert tips will guide you through the process, ensuring delicious results that will impress your family and friends.

Freeze drying isn't just confined to the kitchen; its applications extend far beyond culinary pursuits. We explore the myriad ways freeze-drying is transforming industries and lifestyles around the globe. From pharmaceuticals and biotechnology to the preservation of historical artifacts and floral arrangements, freeze-drying plays a vital role in preserving and enhancing various materials. We'll delve into these diverse applications, highlighting the ingenuity and innovation driving the evolution of freeze-drying technology.

As with any culinary endeavor, mastering the art of freeze-drying requires practice, patience, and a willingness to learn. We offer valuable tips and tricks from our experiences to help you achieve freeze-drying perfection. From proper storage techniques to troubleshooting common issues, we'll equip you with the knowledge and expertise needed to overcome challenges and unleash the full potential of freeze-drying in your culinary creations.

We invite you to embrace the endless possibilities that this innovative preservation method offers. From enriching flavors and extending shelf life to revolutionizing industries, freeze-drying has truly transformed the way we interact with food and beyond. So, let's embark on this culinary adventure together, exploring, experimenting, and savoring the remarkable world of freeze-dried delights. Cheers to culinary innovation, preservation, and endless gastronomic adventures!

Chapter One

Freeze-Drying Basics

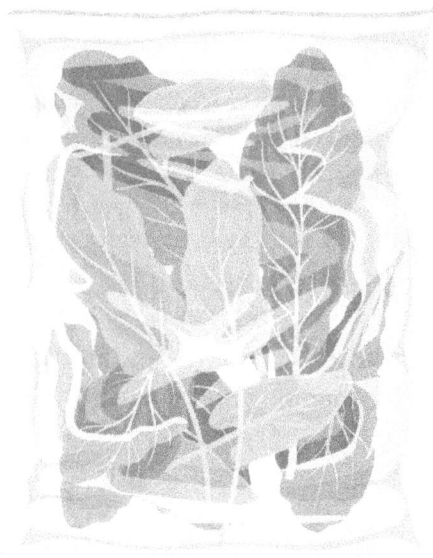

Welcome to the world of freeze-drying basics, where you'll learn all you need to know about this cool way (pun fully intended) to preserve and store foods. In this chapter, we'll look at a few basics you should know - from all the equipment you need to a few important things that could affect drying times.

Ready? Let's jump straight in.

Equipment

Using the right equipment for the job will help your food keep well, sealing in all the nutrients and goodness for a long time. Here are a few things you will need to start your drying process.

A Freeze Dryer

An electric freeze dryer is your ideal companion for drying foods. It controls both the temperature and air so that your food dries just right every time. It's easy to use and can even be used by beginners who have never used one before. It's simple: stack your foods on the handy trays inside the freeze dryer, and it does the rest for you.

Of course, like any electrical appliance, wattage, fan speed, the amount of airflow, and drying trays vary according to price. So, while cheaper models can do a good job, a more expensive model with more features will do even better. For more information on this, pick up my first book, **"Freeze Drying Mastery For Beginners."**

Controlling the Temperature

Most home electric freeze dryers have a temperature range of -20 to -40°F, which will dry everything from meat jerky to vegetables and herbs. The operating room temperature should be between 50 and 75°F. If this is your first time using a freeze dryer, or you have purchased one for a specific occasion (like that annual camping trip you take with your family every fall), a basic model with fewer functions might be just what you need. If you place frozen products into your freeze dryer, your machine will cool them even further to around -40 degrees F.

If you are looking for a food freeze dryer with excellent temperature control settings, an array of functions, and additional drying trays, you can expect to pay a little more for your dehydrator. Sure, spending that extra cash may seem daunting, but it is worth it when you consider the temperature control settings.

Freeze Drying Trays

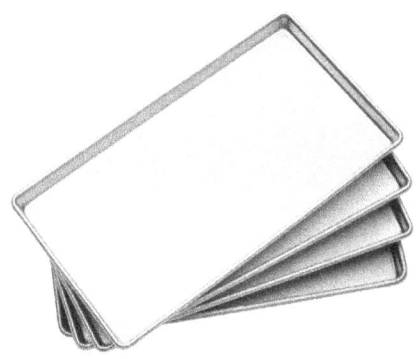

Image Credit: www.HarvestRight.com

Freezing trays are an important component of your freeze dryer and have an open grid to allow for airflow. Depending on the make and model of your specific dryer, you can expect the trays to be made from either plastic or stainless steel - usually between one and one and a half inches thick. These trays are ideal for drying meats, fruits, larger herbs, and vegetables (or anything, really).

For smaller foods, like berries, baby potatoes, and smaller pieces of meats, a mesh tray is ideal. Again, depending on the make and model of your freeze dryer, these might come as a standard accessory or can be purchased as an optional extra.

If you're drying puree or mashed potatoes, you will need to use a solid liner in your dryer. These are optional accessories or might be included in your freeze dryer. Recipes that call for a solid liner will often refer to this in the instructions as a "lined drying tray."

Remember to rotate your drying trays every few hours to ensure that your foods are drying evenly.

Knives and Blades: The Cutting Tools You'll Need

A drying job is only possible with a few essential cutting tools. From chopping and slicing to paring and peeling, here are the most important knives to prepare your foods for freeze-drying.

Chef's Knife

Invest in a good-quality chef's knife with a blade of at least 8- to 10-inches. This is the ideal size for chopping and slicing all the foods you want to dry.

Paring Knife

We all own a paring knife, but we often forget that it is a great little knife for smaller tasks like coring an apple, trimming extra fat from meat, and even hulling strawberries.

Vegetable Peeler

A vegetable peeler is a versatile little tool that is ideal for peeling potatoes, butternut, and carrots.

Serrated Utility Knife

This handy little cutting tool is great for evenly slicing tomatoes, fruits, and even vegetables for drying purposes.

Adjustable Slicer

A mandoline or adjustable slicer is ideal for beginners to cut their vegetables and fruits into even slices. It can also be used to shred or dice fruits and vegetables.

Food Processor

No kitchen is complete without an electric food processor or hand-held mixer. These can be used to puree or mash foods before drying.

If you don't already have these in your kitchen, you might want to invest in a few or all of these to help you prepare your foods for freeze-drying.

Other Tools You Might Need

Aside from the more obvious tools you will need, like knives and food processors, there are a few more tools that will help make preparing your foods for freeze-drying just that much easier:

- Cutting boards
- A colander
- Large bowls
- Baking sheets or silicone baking trays
- Cloths and paper towels
- Stainers
- Disposable gloves
- A steamer
- Hand or stick blender

The best advice that we can give you is to use whatever you have to make preparation easier and fuss-free. So use that apple corer, banana or bean slicer, meat grinder, or vegetable brush and prepare your meats, fruits, and vegetables quickly and easily.

Best Practices for Efficient and Safe Freeze Drying

Whether you're preserving fruits and vegetables or making delicious snacks like beef jerky, it's important to follow the proper guidelines to ensure the best results while keeping your foods safe for consumption later.

In this section, let's look at a few essential tips that you should consider to help you sanitize your surfaces, choose your higher-quality foods, and make sure your space stays as clean as possible during the drying process.

So, let's jump right in and see just what the best practices are for safe freeze-drying.

Cleanliness is Key

One of the most important aspects of preparing your foods for drying is to maintain cleanliness from start to finish. Here are a few useful tips you can follow:

- Always clean and sanitize your work area and all tools that you will be using. This includes all knives, peelers, bowls, and other tools you will be using to prepare your foods for drying.

- Wash your hands before, during, and after the preparation process.

- Wear gloves if you have any sores or cuts on your hands or fingers. This minimizes the risk of contaminating your foods and reduces the risk of infection.

Choosing Your Foods

Choosing foods to freeze dry is a fairly simple process when you follow these fantastic tips:

- Choose foods that are in as perfect a condition as possible.

- Fruits, vegetables, and meat should be stored in the refrigerator until they are prepared or ready to be put in the freezer.

- Fruits and vegetables with soft spots of bruises should not be freeze-dried, as they could contain bacteria.

- Always wash your produce thoroughly before cutting and slicing it.

- Choosing meats should be done with care. Lean cuts of meat, like loin, flank, and round meats, are ideal for drying and take less time. Fat, while often tasty on jerky, will only turn rancid when freeze-dried.

- Pork should always be frozen before being dried. This is to kill the Trichinella Spiralis parasite that could be present in raw pork. Remember to thaw it in the refrigerator.

- Aged or ground meats will contain higher levels of bacteria, so precook or pretreat them if you are making jerky. The same can be said for wild game, which needs to be precooked to destroy harmful pathogens.

Safety Tips for Using Your Freeze Dryer

Want to make the most of your freeze dryer? Here are a few tips that can help you up your game:

- Preheat your dryer before placing your food on the drying trays. By preheating your freeze dryer for as little as 10 minutes before using it, you can cut down on drying time, ensure even drying, and help kill off any bacteria that might be in it from storage.

- It is a good idea to place all the drying trays in your freeze dryer, even if you are not going to use them. This maximizes the airflow, ensuring faster and more consistent drying.

- Don't overload your drying trays. Foods should be evenly spaced across the entire tray. Place moist or dense foods apart to maximize the airflow.

Your Freeze-Dried Foods

Once you have dried your foods, there are certain things you can do to ensure that they last for a long time. Here are a few tips:

- Check for excessive moisture after drying your foods. Moisture will cause your foods to go rancid.
- Seal your dried foods in a clean, airtight container, and always store them in a cool, dark place.
- Store foods in portions where possible. Small batches are better to avoid introducing moisture.
- All freeze-dried foods should be checked for moisture monthly. If your food shows any signs of moisture, simply re-dry them.
- Mold is a big no-no for dried foods. If you find even the smallest spot of mold in any containers of freeze-dried food, discard the batch and wash your container thoroughly.

Pretreatments

Pretreating certain foods before drying them helps ensure that they turn out just right. It can also keep food tasting good, looking great, and, most importantly, making it safe to eat. Pretreating is essential to stop certain enzymes from causing your foods to change color or taste and can help get rid of any germs that might be on or in your foods.

Let's look at a few of the more popular pretreatment methods you can use for your freeze-dried foods.

Why Pretreat Foods Before Freeze Drying?

Here are a few more benefits of pretreating your foods:

- Prevents light-colored vegetables and fruits from browning
- Kills off all enzymes that lead to spoilage in vegetables
- Ensures your foods dry evenly, improving their storage life significantly
- Reduces microbe action

Blanching

This pretreatment method involves placing food on a rack over boiling water rather than in it. Remember to cover your pot tightly and time the blanching process carefully.

Blanching time depends not only on the type of foods you are drying but also on the size of the pieces of food. You can test your blanched foods by cutting through a piece to see if it is "tender-crisp." It should still be crunchy in the center and more tender towards the outside. Do remember that blanching time in recipes depends on not only the size of the pieces but also the types of food you are pretreating before placing them in your freeze dryer.

After you have blanched your foods, drain them, pat them dry with a cloth or paper towel, and place them in your dryer immediately.

Water Blanching

Water blanching is a popular method for pretreating foods before dehydrating them. It involves briefly immersing fruits or vegetables in water. This is an ideal pretreatment method for firmer-skinned fruits like grapes, plums, cranberries, and blueberries. It is done to open the pores on the fruit's skin. It is also known as "crazing" or "checking."

This process is not only quick but also helps your fruit dry evenly when placed in a freeze-dryer. Again, after water blanching, remember to drain your fruit, pat it dry, and place it in your freeze-dryer immediately.

Acidulating

Did you know that certain acids can help prevent vegetables and fruits from browning during the freeze-drying process by deactivating the enzymes that cause oxidation?

Here are a few ideas of the acids you can use to acidulate your fruits and vegetables. Simply soak your preferred food in any of these solutions for 5 minutes, drain, pat dry, and place in your freeze-dryer immediately:

1. **Vitamin C tablets of ascorbic acid**: These are available from any drugstore. To prepare your solution, crush 6 x 500mg tablets and dissolve in 1 gallon of water.
2. **Bottled or freshly squeezed 100% fruit juice**: Soak your fruits and vegetables in the fresh fruit juice of your choice.
3. **Antioxidants**: These are available for commercial use and should be used according to the directions on the packaging.
4. **Citric acid powder**: Citric acid powder is a fantastic solution for acidifying fruits and vegetables for freeze-drying. Simply dissolve 5g of the powder in 1 quart of fresh water.

Sugar Syrups

It's a well-known fact that sugar slows down the browning process in fruit. While it is not quite as effective as acidulating your fruits, using a sugar syrup has the added bonus of making your fruits sweet and plump after the freeze-drying process.

Sugar syrups are so simple to make. Here's how:

- **For a medium syrup:** Dissolve ⅓ cup sugar in ¾ cup water
- **For a heavy syrup:** Dissolve ½ cup sugar in ¾ cup water
- **For a very heavy syrup:** Dissolve ⅔ cup sugar in ¾ cup water

Syrup strength is really a matter of personal preference, so choose the option that works for you. If you prefer a "healthier" option, you can substitute half the sugar for honey.

To use your sugar or honey solution to pretreat your fruits, simply simmer your preferred fruits in the solution for 1 to 2 minutes. Turn off the heat completely and let the fruit stand for up to 30 minutes. It should be cool enough to handle. Once cooled, simmer, drain, and pat your fruit dry before placing it into the freeze-dryer.

Salt Solutions

Salt solutions are another popular pretreatment option that helps prevent and reduce the growth of microbes in the meats, vegetables, and fruit that you are going to dehydrate. Here's how to use it:

For fruits or vegetables:

Dissolve 2 to 4 tablespoons of regular table salt, or kosher salt if you prefer, in 1 gallon of water and soak your fruits and vegetables for at least 5 minutes.

For meats:

Meats require a bit more salt than fruits and vegetables do. For meat, you will need to dissolve ½ to ⅔ cup of table/canning/pickling salt in 1 quart of fresh water. If you prefer kosher salt, you will need to dissolve ¾ cup of kosher salt into 1 quart of fresh water. Place your meat in the solution and soak for between 4 and 24 hours, depending on your meat's thickness and how salty you want it to be. Remember to place your meat and salt solution in the refrigerator.

After soaking, drain your fruit, vegetables, or meat, pat them dry, and immediately place them on your freeze-drying trays.

Sodium Nitrite

The last pretreatment on our list is sodium nitrite. While this may sound more like a science experiment than a pretreatment to reduce microbial growth when dehydrating meats, it is perfectly safe when used according to the package instructions.

The most popular sodium nitrates, also known as curing salts, are cure #1, pink salt, TCM, InstaCure No. 1, DC Curing Salt, DQ Curing Salt, and Heller's Modern Cure. These mixes are available online and in stores that sell meat-curing and dehydrating supplies.

Pre-Freezing

Yes, pre-freezing your foods can help cut down on drying time. Pre-freezing also speeds up the drying process by creating smaller ice crystals that ensure even freezing.

When is Dry, Dry Enough?

You might be asking yourself just how dry is dry enough when freeze-drying your foods. Well, it really depends on the type of foods you are drying, what you will be using them for, and also on personal preference. In terms of drying, it is important to remember that drying too dry is much better than not drying enough.

Let's look at a few important guidelines you should consider when freeze-drying foods and also ensuring that they are adequately dry:

Fruit and Meat

Fruits and meat freeze-dried as a snack should be dried until they are "leathery" and "flexible." But just what does this mean? Let's look at the definitions of these two terms.

Leathery means that your dried fruit or meat should peel away from the drying tray easily and not be sticky at all.

Flexibility, on the other hand, means that your meat or fruit should not break when bent and show no visible moisture when cut or squeezed.

It is important to remember that there will be exceptions to the rules above, though, especially when using high-sugar fruits that may feel slightly sticky even after dehydrating - like cherries and figs.

Here are a few more tips on how to know when your fruits and meats are properly dried:

- Fruit purees should be dried to what is known as "flexible leather" and should be firm with no sticky or soft spots. They should also peel easily from the drying tray in one piece while warm.

- Vegetables dried to make chips should be crisp and rattle when shaken.

- Chopped and sliced vegetables that will be used in any of the recipes we will share later in this book should also be dried until they rattle.

- Herbs should be dried until they are brittle. This seals in the flavor.

Storing Dried Foods: A Drying Guide

The way you store your foods will also affect the way that you dry them. Here are a few tips you should follow according to your preferred storage method:

- To store dried foods for longer, freeze-dry them until they break apart easily and are brittle.

- Dry fruit and vegetables that you want to grind into a powder once dried until they are brittle. They should break apart easily.

- Jerky, made from either meat or fish, is great for snacks and should be dried until pliable, firm, evenly colored, and smooth.

- Vacuum-packed or oxygen-absorbed foods should be dried until they rattle. This includes dried meats and vegetables. Drying them correctly will prevent botulism toxin formation.

Drying meat and vegetables is easy if you know how. But be sure to look out for case hardening. This is then the surface of your meat, vegetable, or fruits forms a tough skin while the inside is still moist. This can be caused by high temperatures, low ambient humidity, or a combination of these two.

Factors Affecting Drying Times

Freeze dryers are fantastic pieces of equipment to own. And, in case you didn't know, drying times can vary considerably—sometimes by hours or even days. Drying time is influenced by a number of factors, and in this section, we'll explore just what these are and what you can do to ensure that you are drying your foods properly.

Here are a few factors that could affect the drying times of your favorite freeze-dried foods:

1. **The type or texture of the foods:**

    Vegetables have a generally airy structure and will dry much faster than dense meats and fruits that tend to hang on to every last drop of moisture.

2. **The size of the foods:**

    Don't be surprised if your thinly sliced apples or tomatoes dry considerably faster than those halved apples, mangoes, or plums.

3. **Pretreatments:**

    Pretreatments like syrup solutions, blanching, acidulating, and marinating tend to add moisture to the foods you want to dry, drastically increasing the drying time.

4. **The relative humidity (RH) of where you are located:**

    Yes, the humidity in the area where you live can affect the drying times of your foods. Drying time is far shorter in dry areas - like those in the desert - where the RH levels are less than 20% or in temperate climates where the RH levels are 40 to 60%.

5. **Freeze Dryer temperatures:**

    It might seem rather obvious, but lower freeze-dryer temperatures will dry food more slowly than those with higher temperatures. This refers not only to the temperature settings but also to the temperature range of your freeze dryer.

6. **The ambient temperatures:**

    The air temperature can also affect drying times. Air temperatures below 70°F are proven to increase drying time. Drying indoors using a freeze dryer is your best bet for drying your foods safely and properly.

A handy tip is to keep a record, a freeze-drying diary, of the foods you dry and how long each one takes to dry. Here are a few ideas of what you can include:

- The size and thickness of each piece of food
- The temperature
- The humidity
- Pretreatments used
- Length of drying time
- Texture of the finished product

Weighing your foods once you have prepared them for drying (after peeling, slicing, etc.) and then again after drying can also be useful information to include in your freeze-drying diary.

Storage: How to Safely Store Freeze-Dried Foods

One of the more important aspects of freeze-drying foods, apart from the proper drying of your foods, of course, is storing them. The way you store your foods can significantly influence how long they last.

There are a few things you can do, and also a few things you should avoid entirely, to safely store your foods, so let's look at a few helpful do's and don'ts of safe food storage:

- **Do** package your dried foods in airtight containers
- **Don't** use porous packaging
- **Do** store your foods in a cool, dark place
- **Don't** constantly reopen packages
- **Do** store your freeze-dried foods in small batches
- **Don't** store foods in areas of high humidity or in direct light
- **Do** consider using mylar bags with oxygen absorbers, freezing, or vacuum sealing to help extend the storage life of your dried foods

But, How Long Will It Last?

How long your freeze-dried foods last while in storage depends on a few things. One of the main factors is the temperature at which you store them. Simply put, the lower the temperature, the better.

Lower temperatures will increase the storage life of your dried foods. Storing dried foods at 70°F will last for about a month, while those same foods stored at 60, 50, or even 40°F will last for six months to a year. Keeping in mind that room temperature is 70°F, let's look at a few guidelines on how long your freeze-dried foods will last:

- Herbs and brittle, crisp fruits or vegetables = one year
- Pliable and leathery vegetables and fruits = one to three years
- Nuts, grains, and seeds = one to three months
- Dried fish or meat jerky = one to three weeks
- Food mixes, like dried soup mix = as long as the product has the shortest storage life or recommendation

Pro Tip: You can increase your storage times by using pretreatments, refrigerating or freezing your dried foods, using desiccants, and choosing vacuum-sealing or airtight storage options. Remember to check your freeze-dried foods regularly for moisture and pop them back in the dryer if need be.

Storage Options That Work

There are a number of fantastic storage options that you should consider if you really want to make the most of your freeze-dried foods and extend their storage life. From jars and containers to storage bags and vacuum sealing, here are the ins and outs of each option:

Jars and Containers

Glass canning jars, metal containers with lids, and plastic containers are all great options for storing freeze-dried foods and also help keep any bugs or bacteria out of your foods - making them last even longer. But they do require a bit of extra effort to prepare.

Here's how to ensure that your containers are clean, sterilized, and ready to go:

Sterilizing: To sterilize heat-safe jars or metal containers with lids, place them in a large pot of boiling water for at least 10 minutes. Remove with tongs, place on a clean drying rack, and leave to air-dry.

Bleach: You can safely sanitize plastic, metal, and glass containers with bleach by mixing two tablespoons of bleach with at least one gallon of water. Place your storage containers in the bleach solution and soak for two minutes. Remove them from the solution, place them on a clean drying rack, and leave them to air-dry.

Storage Bags

Storage bags are another brilliant option for storing freeze-dried foods. They take up less space, are readily available, and are relatively cheaper to buy than glass, plastic, or metal containers. If appropriately sterilized, storage bags can be used again.

Here's how to ensure that they are clean and ready to use:

New or Unused Bags: These bags do not need to be sterilized before use, and you can simply pop your foods into them and store them as required.

Re-Used Bags: It is perfectly okay to reuse your zip-top bags as long as you clean them. You can either wash them by hand or pop them in the dishwasher. Be careful not to use any abrasive cleaners that might erode the plastic. To sterilize using bleach, simply refer to the guide on how to sterilize jars and containers and follow the same steps.

Vacuum Sealing

Did you know that vacuum sealing your freeze-dried foods can increase their storage time by three to five times? Vacuum sealing involves removing air from your container or plastic bag, creating that all-important air-tight seal. No air means no moisture, microbes, and bacteria from reaching your dried foods, which means they will last far longer.

Vacuum sealers are available at a variety of prices according to their features, so choose one that not only suits your needs but your pocket, too.

Helpful Hints and Tips

Here are a few more tips that you can follow to make the most of your freeze-dried foods and their storage life:

Tip #1: Choose your zip-top bags, jars, or containers to hold portion sizes. Smaller portions mean less opening of your sealed containers.

Tip #2: You can tape over your container lids or use food-safe desiccants to help keep the moisture out. Desiccants are fantastic for absorbing moisture and oxygen, leaving your foods free from microbes and bacteria. A few options of these are:

- Bentonite clay
- Silica
- Calcium Chloride

Tip #3: Alternatively, you can use oxygen absorbers, which are small packets containing iron powder. These handy little packets create a nitrogen-rich environment that helps prevent the growth of any organisms, mold, and insects that cause food spoilage.

Tip #4: Ensure that your dried meats, vegetables, and fruits have dried sufficiently before storing to reduce the risk of botulism poisoning.

Rehydration

Rehydrating your freeze-dried foods is relatively easy. Yes, it simply involves soaking them in water until they are plump and tender again. But how much water should you use? Is there a specific time that you should soak them?

Here are our best tips on how to rehydrate your foods.

Rehydration Times

Rehydration times, like drying times, vary according to the types of food, the rehydration method used, the size of the foods, and their dryness. There are three main rehydration methods.

Cold Soaks

A cold soak is the best option for cold dishes like salads and fruits. It involves soaking your freeze-dried foods in water for half an hour to overnight. Remember to keep your food in the refrigerator if it is going to be soaking for more than 2 hours.

Hot Soaks

Want a fast method for rehydrating your foods? A hot soak is your answer and can be used for most of your freeze-dried foods. Simply pour boiling water over your dried foods, cover your pot with a lid, and let it stand for up to 20 minutes.

Combination Soaks

A combination soak is a great method for meals like soups, stews, or very dry foods that you will be consuming while they are hot. This also saves you on fuel while camping or backpacking. Simply soak your food in cold liquid for 10 to 15 minutes, bring it to a boil, and then reduce the heat. Pop on your pot lid and simmer for another 15 minutes.

Remember to choose the soaking method according to the type and size of the foods you are rehydrating and to keep a close eye on the time.

Equivalents

Sometimes, using freeze-dried foods can be convenient, especially when they are used to replace fresh vegetables or fruits in certain recipes. Here is a guide on just how much to use as a substitute for fresh ingredients in any of the recipes we will share later on in our book.

- **Powders**: 1 to 2 tablespoons
- **Dried and chopped**: 4 to 6 tablespoons
- **Fresh pureed**: 4 to 6 tablespoons
- **Chopped and fresh**: 1 cup
- **Chopped greens**: 1 cup loosely packed (think spinach, parsley, and kale)
- **Fruit or vegetable**: 1 medium to large (apples or onions)
- **Celery stalks**: chopped: 2 to 3 medium
- **Carrots, chopped**: 3 to 4 medium

In the next chapter, we will discuss all the produce you love and how to prep, freeze-dry, and troubleshoot when things don't end up looking right.

Chapter Two

Produce You Will Love

In this jam-packed chapter, we'll explore a few of the more common problems that you might encounter when freeze-drying your foods and give you a few tips on how to fix them for good. Freeze-drying food need not be the challenge you think it is when you know how, and to help you along; we will look at just how to prepare your vegetables and fruits in your freeze-dryer.

Freeze-Dried Food Troubleshooting

When freeze-drying your foods, you might experience a few common problems. But don't panic, as we have the best troubleshooting tips to help make life that much easier. Let's look at a few of the more common problems, a few likely reasons, and also the best tips to fix them.

Problem #1: Your food is not drying, even after 24 hours

There could be a few reasons for this. Here are the most common:

- Some foods take longer to dry than others.
- Results may vary as drying times are usually only given as a guideline.
- The ambient temperature is too high, the room temperature is too cool, and your foods contain too much moisture from blanching or other pretreatments.

Solutions:

- Practice patience with foods that might take longer to dry than others. These include tomato halves, prunes, and other "wet" fruits. This really is all about trial and error, and sometimes, especially in the beginning, there seems to be more error than anything else. Stick with it; you'll get there.
- Preparing your foods in smaller or thinner pieces can cut down on drying time. Then, pat dry with a paper towel to remove any excess moisture.
- Always dry foods at the correct temperature for each type of food you are drying.
- In areas of higher ambient humidity, raise the temperature of the freeze-dryer and, where possible, raise the temperature of the room in colder rooms.

Problem #2: Your freeze-dried food is leathery but still moist inside

There could be a few reasons why your freeze-dried foods are leathery but dry inside. The most common, however, is that your food has case-hardened and needs to be removed from the freeze-dryer.

Solutions:

- Cut your pieces of food in half and place them back in the dehydrator as recommended.

- If your food is still not dry, consider blending it into a paste, placing the paste into the freeze-dryer, and then grinding it into a powder.

- Prepare your foods to prevent case hardening. This includes cutting them into smaller, even pieces and drying them at lower temperatures.

Problem #3: Your fruits aren't drying correctly or become moldy quickly in storage

This is a common problem with waxy fruits like berries, grapes, plums, and cherries. You might just find that these resist drying while in the freeze-dryer.

Solutions:

- Pierce or check the skin of your "waxy" fruits before drying them. This helps moisture to escape.

- Pretreat your fruits by water-blanching them to open up the pores of the skin before you place them in a freeze-dryer.

Problem #4: Your fruits and vegetables have turned brown after drying them

This is a common problem with most fruits and vegetables. This is because they contain enzymes that cause oxidation. This includes apples, bananas, pears, peaches, eggplant, apricots, and even potatoes.

Solutions:

- Pretreat your fruits and vegetables before drying them.

Problem #5: Your vegetables have lost color during freeze-drying

Vegetables often lose their color during the dehydration process. This is only natural as they are exposed to light and heat during storage.

Solutions:

- Pretreating your vegetables by blanching them to deactivate the enzymes that cause oxidation before placing them in a freeze-dryer.

- Store your dried vegetables in a cool, dark, and dry place.

Problem #6: Your dried foods taste absolutely awful

This is not an uncommon problem, and there are a few reasons why your freeze-dried foods do not taste as you would expect them to. Here are a few reasons why:

- The most common reason for this is that different types of food, like meats, fish, fruit, and vegetables, were dried together.
- The foods contained either oil or fat that has now gone rancid.

Solutions:

- Dry your freeze-dried foods separately to prevent flavors and aromas from mixing. This can, however, be done if foods are going to be used together in soups or stews. (like onions, carrots, and beans or peas.)
- If you're making jerky, choose lean cuts of meat that trim off any of the excess fat before pretreatment and drying.

Problem #7: Your freeze-dried food containers contain mold

Mold is a big no-no when it comes to freeze-dried foods, and there is one common reason for this: too much moisture in the packaging or the food was not conditioned or pretreated correctly before drying.

Solutions:

- Condition your foods before storing them to prevent mold build-up.
- Check your stored foods for mold and moisture regularly and re-dry them if any moisture is present.
- Discard any moldy foods immediately.

Problem #8: Your dried foods contain bugs like moths and insects

The reason you are likely finding these little creepy crawlies in your packaged foods is that they haven't been properly packed or stored.

Solutions:

- Clean your pantry shelves and examine your packages for a possible infestation of bugs.
- Always package your dehydrated foods in airtight containers or vacuum-sealed packaging.
- Store your foods in cool, dark, and dry spaces.
- Throw out your dried foods that contain bugs immediately.

Produce You Will Love and How to Prepare Them

This next section will be our ultimate guide to preparing and freeze-drying your favorite fruits and vegetables, so pay close attention to what we share.

Strawberries

Strawberries are relatively soft berries with seeds on the outer surface of the fruit. They are packed with vitamins C and K and rich in antioxidants, making them the perfect snack.

Preparation

To prepare your strawberries for drying, wash and dry them thoroughly, remove the stems, and slice them according to the size you want. Remember that the bigger the strawberry, the longer the drying time. A quick pretreatment with a sugar syrup will help keep the color and help them retain their sweet flavor.

Drying Time and Temperature

Dry your strawberries at -40°F for 24 to 48 hours until firm and dry.

Cherries

Cherries are sweet and juicy pitted fruits that go great on a cake or as a healthy dried snack on the go. They are rich in vitamins C and potassium and can be used in homemade granolas, trail mix, or on their own.

Preparation

To prepare cherries, remove the stems before washing and drying them thoroughly. Remove the pit and place the cherries in a sugar syrup solution to keep their color and provide an even richer flavor. Cherries can be freeze-dried whole, but remember to pierce the skin to ensure proper drying.

Drying Time and Temperature

Cherries should be dried for at least 24 to 48 hours at -40°F or until they are firm and dry.

Raspberries

Raspberries are one of our favorite berries. They are small but super juicy. They make great little dried snacks or can be added to salads for a bit of flavor.

Preparation

To prepare your raspberries, first wash and dry them thoroughly. Soak them in a sugar syrup to pretreat them and ensure that they retain their color and sweet taste.

Drying Time and Temperature

Raspberries should be dried at -40°F for 24 to 48 hours until dry.

Citrus Fruits - Oranges, Limes, Lemons and Grapefruit

Citrus fruits are high in vitamin C, making them great for snacks, making your own teas, and in trail mixes or homemade granola.

Preparation

To prepare them for freeze-drying, wash and dry them well before slicing them evenly. Blanch in water to prevent them from browning.

Drying Time and Temperature

Dry your citrus fruit slices in a freeze-dryer at -40°F for 24 to 48 hours or until dry and leathery.

Grapes

Grapes are sweet and juicy fruits that might contain seeds. They are great on their own or can be added to fruit salads.

Preparation

To prepare your grapes for freeze-drying, remove the stems before washing and drying them thoroughly. Leave them whole, or cut them in half, removing the seeds if there are any.

Drying Time and Temperature

Grapes should be dried at -40°F for at least 24 to 48 hours or until they are shriveled and raisin-like.

Apples

Apples are crisp and sweet fruits that make great dried snacks. Eat them on their own, or add them to trail mix or a homemade granola.

Preparation

To prepare your apples for freeze-drying, wash and dry them and then core them. You can peel them if you prefer. Slice them thinly and soak them in a solution of water and lemon juice to prevent browning.

Drying Time and Temperature

Dry them in a freeze-dryer at -40°F for 24 to 48 hours until they're dry.

Bananas

Bananas are soft and creamy fruits that make a fantastic dried snack. Enjoy them on their own, in a trail mix, or in homemade granola.

Preparation

To prepare bananas for freeze-drying, peel them and slice them into thin rounds. To prevent browning, dip the slices in lemon or pineapple juice.

Drying Time and Temperature

Dry your bananas at -40°F for 24 to 48 hours until they're dry.

Kiwi

Kiwi is a tangy and sweet fruit with fuzzy brown skin. If you've never tasted a dried kiwi, you have to try this method!

Preparation

To prepare for freeze-drying, wash and peel the kiwis. Slice them into thin, even rounds or wedges. Dip the slices in lemon juice to prevent browning.

Drying Time and Temperature

Dry your kiwi slices or wedges in a freeze-dryer at -40°F for 24 to 48 hours until they're dry and slightly chewy.

Apricots

Apricots are soft and juicy fruits with smooth skin. They are incredibly delicious in salads or enjoyed on their own.

Preparation

To prepare apricots for freeze-drying, wash and dry them and slice them in half. Remove the pits. To prevent browning, dip the halves in lemon juice or honey.

Drying Time and Temperature

Dry your halved apricots at -40°F for 24 to 48 hours until they're dry and pliable.

Peaches

Peaches are juicy, sweet fruits with fuzzy skin. Like apricots, they are dried-fruit favorites and can be added to salads for a fresh, slightly tart flavor.

Preparation

To prepare them for freeze-drying, wash and slice them in half. Remove the pits. You can dip the halves in lemon juice or honey to prevent browning.

Drying Time and Temperature

Dry them in a freeze-dryer at -40°F for 24 to 48 hours until they're dry and slightly chewy.

Avocado

Avocado is a creamy fruit with smooth, green skin. While many eat it fresh, avocados can also be freeze-dried, ground, and used in guacamole, as an additive for smoothies, or as a dry snack.

Preparation

To prepare an avocado for freeze-drying, peel and slice it into thin pieces. To prevent browning, dip the slices in lemon juice or vinegar.

Drying Time and Temperature

Dry them in a freeze-dryer at -40°F for 24 to 48 hours until they're leathery and dry.

Cantaloupe

Cantaloupe is a sweet and juicy melon with textured skin. Enjoy it on its own or in a fruit salad, trail mix, or homemade granola.

Preparation

To prepare it for freeze-drying, wash the cantaloupe, remove the seeds, and slice the flesh into thin pieces or cubes.

Drying Time and Temperature

Sliced or cubed cantaloupes should be dried at -40°F for 24 to 48 hours until they are dry and slightly chewy.

Pineapple

Pineapple is a tropical fruit with a tough, spiky skin. This is another fantastic fruit that dries really well, so enjoy it as a snack on its own.

Preparation

To prepare it for freeze-drying, peel the pineapple and slice the flesh into thin pieces or rings. To enhance the flavor, soak the slices in a solution of water and pineapple juice.

Drying Time and Temperature

Dry your pineapple slices or rings at -40°F for 24 to 48 hours until they're dry and chewy.

Plum

Plums are sweet and juicy fruits with smooth skin and a pit inside. They go well paired with dried berries, apricots, and apples as a delicious snack.

Preparation

To prepare it for freeze-drying, wash the plums and slice them in half. Remove the pits, and slice the skin to allow for easy drying. You can dip the halves in lemon juice or honey to prevent browning.

Drying Time and Temperature

Plums can be dried for 24 to 48 hours at -40°F or until they are dry and slightly soft.

Artichokes

Artichokes are a vegetable with a spiky outer layer and a tender heart inside. They can be dried for use in soups and stews.

Preparation

Wash and dry your artichokes thoroughly to prepare them for freeze-drying. Trim off the tough outer leaves and cut off the top and stem. Steam or boil the artichoke until tender, then remove the heart and slice it into pieces.

Drying Time and Temperature

Dry artichokes at -40°F for 24 to 48 hours until they are dry and crisp.

Eggplants

Eggplants are purple vegetables with a spongy texture. They can also be added to stews and soups.

Preparation

To prepare an eggplant for freeze-drying, wash the eggplant and slice it into thin rounds or strips. You can soak the slices in salt water to remove bitterness.

Drying Time and Temperature

Dry your sliced eggplant in a dehydrator at -40°F for 24 to 48 hours until they're dry and leathery.

Asparagus

Asparagus is a green vegetable with long, tender spears. You can dry asparagus to store for use in stews, as a side, or as a delicious dried snack.

Preparation

To prepare it for freeze-drying, wash the asparagus and trim off the tough ends. Blanch the spears in boiling water for a few minutes, then plunge them into ice water to stop the cooking process.

Drying Time and Temperature

Dry your asparagus spears at -40°F for 24 to 48 hours until they're dry and brittle.

Broccoli

Broccoli is a green vegetable with small, floret-like heads. Dried broccoli is great for use in soups and stews.

Preparation

To prepare it for freeze-drying, wash the broccoli and cut it into bite-sized pieces. Blanch the pieces in boiling water for a few minutes, then plunge them into ice water to stop the cooking process.

Drying Time and Temperature

Dry your broccoli pieces in a dehydrator at -40°F for 24 to 48 hours until they're dry and crunchy.

Brussels Sprouts

Brussels sprouts are small, green vegetables that grow in clusters on a stalk.

Preparation

To prepare them for freeze-drying, wash the Brussels sprouts and trim off the tough ends. Cut them in half lengthwise. Blanch the halves in boiling water for a few minutes, then plunge them into ice water to stop the cooking process.

Drying Time and Temperature

Dry them in a freeze-dryer at -40°F for 24 to 48 hours until they're dry and crispy.

Cabbage

Cabbage is a leafy vegetable with thick, crunchy leaves. It also dries really well and can be added to stews or soups or made into purees.

Preparation

To prepare it for freeze-drying, wash the cabbage and remove the tough outer leaves. Shred or slice the cabbage into thin strips. Blanch the strips in boiling water for a few minutes, then plunge them into ice water to stop the cooking process.

Drying Time and Temperature

Dry them in a freeze-dryer at -40°F for 24 to 48 hours until they're dry and crisp.

Kohlrabi

Kohlrabi is a bulbous vegetable with a tough outer layer and crisp white flesh inside. Like carrots, Kohlrabi makes a delicious snack when dried and can be added to soups and stews.

Preparation

To prepare Kohlrabi for freeze-drying, wash the kohlrabi and peel off the outer layer. Slice the flesh into thin rounds or strips. Blanch the slices in boiling water for a few minutes, then plunge them into ice water to stop the cooking process.

Drying Time and Temperature

Dry them in a freeze-dryer at -40°F for 24 to 48 hours until they're dry and leathery.

Squash

Squash is a versatile vegetable with soft, edible flesh and seeds inside. Dehydrate squash to make a puree, or add it to soups and stews for incredible flavor.

Preparation

To prepare it for freeze-drying, wash the squash and cut it into slices or cubes, removing the seeds if desired. You can blanch the slices in boiling water for a few minutes to soften them slightly.

Drying Time and Temperature

Dry your cubed squash in a freeze-dryer at -40°F for 24 to 48 hours until they're dry and slightly chewy.

Peas

Peas are small, round vegetables with a sweet flavor and tender texture. When dried and rehydrated well, they make great little snacks.

Preparation

To prepare them for freeze-drying, wash the peas and remove them from the pods. Blanch the peas in boiling water for a few minutes, then plunge them into ice water to stop the cooking process.

Drying Time and Temperature

Dry your peas at -40°F for 24 to 48 hours until they're dry and crunchy.

Cauliflower

Cauliflower is a white vegetable with a dense, floret-like head. For some, it can be a delicious snack when dried and seasoned.

Preparation

To prepare a cauliflower for freeze-drying, wash and dry it, and then cut it into bite-sized florets. Blanch the florets in boiling water for a few minutes, then plunge them into ice water to stop the cooking process.

Drying Time and Temperature

Dry your cauliflower chunks at -40°F for 24 to 48 hours until they're dry and crisp.

Spinach

Spinach is a leafy green vegetable. Dehydrate it for purees, as a snack, or to be added to a salad.

Preparation

To prepare it for freeze-drying, wash the spinach leaves and pat them dry. Spread them out on freeze-drying trays in a single layer.

Drying Time and Temperature

Dry spinach at -40°F for 24 to 48 hours until it is dry and crispy.

Ginger

Ginger is a knobby root with a spicy flavor. It can be used in soups, teas, and stir-fries.

Preparation

To prepare it for freeze-drying, peel the ginger and slice it thinly. Lay the slices on freeze-drying trays.

Drying Time and Temperature

Dry at -40°F for 24 to 48 hours until your ginger is dry and brittle.

Bean Sprouts

Bean sprouts are crunchy sprouts from beans or seeds. Toss dried bean sprouts in a salad or eat them as a snack for an exciting burst of flavor.

Preparation

To prepare bean sprouts for drying, rinse the bean sprouts thoroughly and pat them dry. Spread them out on freeze-drying trays.

Drying Time and Temperature

Dry your bean sprouts at -40°F for 24 to 48 hours until they're dry and crispy.

Beetroot

Beetroot is a sweet and earthy root vegetable. If you've ever enjoyed beetroot crisps, this method is quick and easy to do at home.

Preparation

To prepare it for freeze-drying, wash the beetroot and peel it. Slice it thinly or grate it. Lay the slices or grated pieces on freeze-drying trays.

Drying Time and Temperature

Dry your crisps at -40°F for 24 to 48 hours until they're dry and leathery.

Bell Peppers

Bell peppers are sweet and crunchy vegetables. Dehydrate them to add to salads and stir fry.

Preparation

To prepare them for freeze-drying, wash the peppers and remove the stems, seeds, and membranes. Slice the peppers into strips or rings. Lay the slices on freeze-drying trays.

Drying Time and Temperature

Dry your sliced bell peppers at -40°F for 24 to 48 hours until they're dry and slightly chewy.

Calabrese (Broccoli)

Calabrese, also known as broccoli, is a green vegetable with a dense, floret-like head. Like regular broccoli, it can be frozen-dried as a snack or for soups and stews.

Preparation

To prepare it for freeze-dryer, wash the broccoli and cut it into bite-sized florets. Blanch the florets in boiling water for a few minutes, then plunge them into ice water to stop the cooking process.

Drying Time and Temperature

Dry your Calabrese at -40°F for 24 to 48 hours until they're dry and crispy.

Potato

Potatoes are starchy root vegetables with a multitude of uses. From crisps to mash to roast potatoes, you simply can't go wrong with this vegetable.

Preparation

To prepare it for freeze-drying, wash the potatoes and peel them if desired. Slice them into thin rounds or strips, and lay the slices or strips on dehydrator trays.

Drying Time and Temperature

Dry your potatoes at -40°F for 24 to 48 hours until they're dry and crispy.

Sweetcorn

Sweetcorn is a sweet and juicy vegetable. Dried sweetcorn is great as a snack or can be added to salads.

Preparation

To prepare it for freeze-drying, wash the sweetcorn and remove the kernels from the cob. Spread the kernels out on freeze-drying trays.

Drying Time and Temperature

Dry corn kernels at -40°F for 24 to 48 hours until they're dry and slightly chewy.

Carrots

Carrots are crunchy and sweet root vegetables. Carrots can be eaten dry as a snack, added to a salad, or used in soups and stews.

Preparation

To prepare the carrots for freeze-drying, wash and peel them. Slice them into thin rounds or strips, and lay the slices or strips on freeze-drying trays.

Drying Time and Temperature

Dry carrot strips or slices at -40°F for 24 to 48 hours until they're dry and slightly chewy.

Green Beans

Green beans are crunchy and flavorful vegetables. Dried green beans can be added to stews or salads and rehydrated to be served as a side.

Before we move to the next chapter, I have a favor to ask. If you have enjoyed this book so far, please take 2 minutes of your time and leave me your honest review on Amazon. It will go a long way in helping others who are looking for this type of information find it easier. Your review makes a huge difference, so please take the time to do it; it means a lot to me.

Preparation

To prepare green beans for drying, wash them and trim them off the ends. Blanch the beans in boiling water for a few minutes, then plunge them into ice water to stop the cooking process.

Drying Time and Temperature

Dry your green beans at -40°F for 24 to 48 hours until they're dry and slightly chewy.

Garlic

Garlic is a pungent bulb with a strong flavor. It has a multitude of uses, including in sauces, stews, and to flavor meats and vegetables.

Preparation

To prepare your garlic for freeze-drying, peel the garlic cloves and slice them thinly. Lay the slices on freeze-drying trays.

Drying Time and Temperature

Dry your garlic cloves at -40°F for 24 to 48 hours until they're dry and crispy.

Tomato

Tomato is a juicy and flavorful fruit. It can be used in salads and stews.

Preparation

To prepare fresh tomatoes for freeze-drying, wash them and slice them thinly. Then, lay the slices on freeze-drying trays.

Drying Time and Temperature

Dry tomato slices at -40°F for 24 to 48 hours until they're dry and slightly chewy.

Cucumber

Cucumber is a crisp and refreshing vegetable. It is great in salads and provides a fresh taste.

Preparation

To prepare it for freeze-drying, wash the cucumber and slice it thinly. If you prefer, you can peel it before slicing. Lay the slices on freeze-drying trays.

Drying Time and Temperature

Dry your slices of cucumber at -40°F for 24 to 48 hours until they're dry and crispy.

As you will learn, drying fruits and vegetables is relatively easy. Remember to check your vegetables often while drying to ensure that they are drying evenly, and adjust the drying time as needed. In the next chapter, we will jump right into delicious recipes. Start experimenting, and remember to have fun!

Chapter Three

For The Vegetarian In You

Coconut Curry Ramen

SERVINGS: 4   **PREP TIME:** 20 MIN   **COOK TIME:** 20 MIN   **FREEZE-DRY TIME:** 24-48 HRS

Ingredients:

2 (3 oz) packages dried ramen noodles (discard spice packet)
8 oz mushrooms, sliced (cremini or shiitake)
1 lime, juiced
2 baby bok choy, chopped
1 tablespoon canola oil
4 cups vegetable broth
1 can (13.5 oz) coconut milk
2 tablespoons red curry paste
2 tablespoons soy sauce
1 tablespoon ginger, grated
1 clove garlic, minced

Optional toppings: sliced green onions, sesame seeds, chili flakes

Instructions:

1. In a large pot, heat the canola oil over medium heat. Add the garlic and ginger, sautéing until fragrant.
2. Stir in the red curry paste, then add the vegetable broth, coconut milk, and soy sauce and bring to a simmer.
3. Add the mushrooms and baby bok choy, and cook until tender.
4. Cook the ramen noodles according to package instructions, then drain and add to the pot. Stir in lime juice.
5. Serve hot with optional toppings as desired.

For Freeze-Drying:

- **Prepare**: After cooking, allow the ramen to cool completely.
- **Freeze**: Spread the ramen mixture on freeze-dryer trays in an even layer.
- **Freeze Dry**: Freeze-dry the curry ramen at -40°F for 24 to 48 hours until completely dry.
- **Store**: Once dry, store the freeze-dried ramen in airtight containers or mylar bags with oxygen absorbers.

Rehydrating:

- **Rehydrate**: To rehydrate, add hot water to the freeze-dried ramen gradually until reaching your desired consistency. Stir well.
- **Serve**: Allow it to sit for a few minutes to fully absorb the water, then enjoy your rehydrated coconut curry ramen.

Crock-Pot Vegetable Lasagna

SERVINGS: 4   **PREP TIME:** 20 MIN   **COOK TIME:** 4-6 HRS   **FREEZE-DRY TIME:** 24-48 HRS

Ingredients:

- 9 lasagna noodles
- 2 cups marinara sauce
- 1 cup ricotta cheese
- 1 cup shredded mozzarella cheese
- 1 cup grated Parmesan cheese
- 2 cups mixed vegetables (such as spinach, mushrooms, zucchini, bell peppers, and onions), chopped
- 2 cloves garlic, minced
- 1 teaspoon dried basil
- 1 teaspoon dried oregano

Salt and pepper to taste

Instructions:

1. In a bowl, mix together the ricotta cheese, half of the mozzarella cheese, half of the Parmesan cheese, minced garlic, dried basil, dried oregano, salt, and pepper.
2. Spread a thin layer of marinara sauce on the bottom of your Crock-Pot.
3. Place three lasagna noodles on top of the marinara sauce, breaking them if needed to fit.
4. Spread half of the ricotta cheese mixture over the noodles.
5. Layer half of the mixed vegetables on top of the ricotta cheese mixture.
6. Repeat the layers: marinara sauce, lasagna noodles, remaining ricotta cheese mixture, and remaining mixed vegetables.
7. Finish with a final layer of marinara sauce and sprinkle the remaining mozzarella and Parmesan cheese on top.
8. Cover the Crock-Pot and cook on low for 4-6 hours or until the noodles are tender and the cheese is melted and bubbly.
9. Once cooked, let the lasagna cool slightly before serving.

For Freeze-Drying:

- **Prepare**: After cooking, allow the vegetable lasagna to cool completely. Cut the lasagna into serving-sized portions.
- **Freeze**: Place the portions on freeze-drying trays, making sure they're not touching each other.
- **Freeze Dry**: Dry the lasagna at -40°F for 24 to 48 hours until completely dry.
- **Store**: Once dry, remove the freeze-dried lasagna from the trays and store them in airtight containers or vacuum-sealed bags.

Rehydrating:

- **Rehydrate**: Place a portion in a bowl or dish. Add enough hot water to cover the lasagna completely. Let the lasagna soak in the hot water for about 10-15 minutes, stirring occasionally, until fully rehydrated and heated through.
- **Serve**: Drain any excess water, if necessary, and enjoy your rehydrated vegetable lasagna!

Roasted Cauliflower Tacos

SERVINGS: 4   **PREP TIME:** 20 MIN   **COOK TIME:** 25 MIN   **FREEZE-DRY TIME:** 24-48 HRS

Ingredients:

1 head cauliflower, cut into florets
2 tablespoons olive oil
1 tablespoon chili powder
1 teaspoon ground cumin
1/2 teaspoon paprika
1/2 teaspoon garlic powder
1/4 teaspoon onion powder
Salt and pepper to taste
8 small corn tortillas

Toppings: shredded cabbage, diced tomatoes, sliced avocado, chopped cilantro, lime wedges, salsa, sour cream (optional)

Instructions:

1. Preheat your oven to 425°F.
2. In a large bowl, toss the cauliflower florets with olive oil, chili powder, cumin, paprika, garlic powder, onion powder, salt, and pepper until evenly coated.
3. Spread the cauliflower in a single layer on a baking sheet lined with parchment paper.
4. Roast the cauliflower in the preheated oven for 20-25 minutes or until tender and golden brown, flipping halfway through cooking.
5. While the cauliflower is roasting, warm the corn tortillas in a dry skillet over medium heat for about 1 minute on each side or until soft and pliable.
6. Assemble the tacos by filling each tortilla with roasted cauliflower and your desired toppings.
7. Serve the tacos with lime wedges on the side for squeezing.

For Freeze-Drying:

- **Prepare**: Allow the roasted cauliflower tacos to cool completely after assembling. Carefully wrap each taco individually in plastic wrap or foil to prevent freezer burn.
- **Freeze**: Place the wrapped tacos on freeze-drying trays, making sure they're not touching each other.
- **Freeze Dry**: Freeze dry the tacos at -40°F for 24 to 48 hours until completely dry.
- **Store**: Once dry, remove the freeze-dried tacos from the trays and store them in airtight containers or vacuum-sealed bags.

Rehydrating:

- **Rehydrate**: To rehydrate the freeze-dried tacos, unwrap them and place them in a bowl or dish. Add enough hot water to cover the tacos completely. Let the tacos soak in the hot water for about 10-15 minutes, stirring occasionally, until fully rehydrated and heated through.
- **Serve**: Drain any excess water, if necessary, and enjoy your rehydrated roasted cauliflower tacos with your favorite toppings!

Creamy Roasted Red Pepper Pasta

SERVINGS: 4   **PREP TIME:** 10 MIN   **COOK TIME:** 45 MIN   **FREEZE-DRY TIME:** 24-48 HRS

Ingredients:

- 12 oz (340g) pasta (such as penne or fettuccine)
- 2 large red bell peppers
- 2 tablespoons olive oil
- 2 cloves garlic, minced
- 1 onion, finely chopped
- 1 cup (240ml) vegetable broth
- 1 cup (240ml) heavy cream
- 1/2 cup (50g) grated Parmesan cheese
- Salt and pepper to taste
- Fresh basil leaves for garnish (optional)

Instructions:

1. Preheat your oven to 450°F.
2. Cut the red bell peppers in half and remove the seeds and membranes.
3. Place the pepper halves, cut side down, on a baking sheet lined with parchment paper.
4. Roast the peppers in the preheated oven for 20-25 minutes or until the skins are blistered and charred.
5. Remove the peppers from the oven and transfer them to a bowl. Cover the bowl with plastic wrap and let the peppers steam for about 10 minutes.
6. Once cooled, peel off the skins from the peppers and discard them. Chop the roasted peppers into small pieces and set aside.
7. Cook the pasta according to the package instructions until al dente. Drain and set aside.
8. In a large skillet, heat the olive oil over medium heat. Add the minced garlic and chopped onion, and sauté until softened and fragrant, about 3-4 minutes.
9. Add the chopped roasted red peppers to the skillet and stir to combine.
10. Pour in the vegetable broth and bring to a simmer. Let it cook for about 5 minutes.
11. Transfer the mixture to a blender or food processor and blend until smooth.
12. Return the blended mixture to the skillet. Stir in the heavy cream and grated Parmesan cheese until well combined. Season with salt and pepper to taste.
13. Add the cooked pasta to the skillet and toss until evenly coated with the creamy red pepper sauce.
14. Cook for an additional 2-3 minutes or until heated through.
15. Serve the creamy roasted red pepper pasta garnished with fresh basil leaves, if desired.

For Freeze-Drying:

- **Prepare:** Allow the creamy roasted red pepper pasta to cool completely after cooking. Portion the pasta into serving-sized portions.
- **Freeze:** Place the portions on freeze-drying trays, making sure they're not touching each other.
- **Freeze Dry:** Freeze dry the pasta at -40°F for 24 to 48 hours until completely dry.
- **Store:** Once dry, remove the freeze-dried pasta from the trays and store them in airtight containers or vacuum-sealed bags.

Rehydrating:

- **Rehydrate:** To rehydrate the freeze-dried pasta, place a portion in a bowl or dish. Add enough hot water to cover the pasta completely. Let the pasta soak in the hot water for about 10-15 minutes, stirring occasionally, until fully rehydrated and heated through.
- **Serve:** Drain any excess water, if necessary, and enjoy your rehydrated creamy roasted red pepper pasta!

Beans Bourguignon

SERVINGS: 4   **PREP TIME:** 15 MIN   **COOK TIME:** 60 MIN   **FREEZE-DRY TIME:** 24-48 HRS

Ingredients:

- 2 tablespoons olive oil
- 1 onion, chopped
- 2 cloves garlic, minced
- 2 carrots, diced
- 2 stalks celery, diced
- 8 oz (225g) mushrooms, sliced
- 2 tablespoons tomato paste
- 1 cup (240ml) red wine
- 2 cups (480ml) vegetable broth
- 2 bay leaves
- 1 teaspoon dried thyme
- Salt and pepper to taste
- 2 cans (15 oz each) of cooked beans (such as kidney beans or cannellini beans), drained and rinsed
- **Fresh parsley for garnish (optional)**

Instructions:

1. Heat the olive oil in a large pot over medium heat.
2. Add the chopped onion, minced garlic, diced carrots, and diced celery to the pot. Sauté until the vegetables are softened, about 5-7 minutes.
3. Add the sliced mushrooms to the pot and cook until they release their moisture and begin to brown about 5 minutes.
4. Stir in the tomato paste and cook for another 2 minutes.
5. Pour in the red wine and simmer for 5 minutes, allowing the alcohol to cook off.
6. Add the vegetable broth, bay leaves, dried thyme, salt, and pepper to the pot. Stir to combine.
7. Bring the mixture to a boil, then reduce the heat to low and let it simmer for 20-30 minutes, allowing the flavors to meld together and the sauce to thicken.
8. Stir in the cooked beans and cook for an additional 10 minutes or until heated through.
9. Taste and adjust the seasoning with more salt and pepper if needed.
10. Remove the bay leaves from the pot before serving.
11. Garnish the Beans Bourguignon with fresh parsley, if desired.

For Freeze-Drying:

- **Prepare**: Allow the Beans Bourguignon to cool completely after cooking. Portion the dish into serving-sized portions.
- **Freeze**: Place the portions on freeze-drying trays, making sure they're not touching each other.
- **Freeze Dry**: Freeze dry the Beans Bourguignon at -40°F for 24 to 48 hours until completely dry.
- **Store**: Once dry, remove the freeze-dried dish from the trays and store them in airtight containers or vacuum-sealed bags.

Rehydrating:

- **Rehydrate**: To rehydrate the freeze-dried Beans Bourguignon, place a portion in a bowl or dish. Add enough hot water to cover the dish completely. Let the dish soak in the hot water for about 10-15 minutes, stirring occasionally, until fully rehydrated and heated through.
- **Serve**: Drain any excess water, if necessary, and enjoy your rehydrated Beans Bourguignon!

Vegan Mac N "Cheeze"

SERVINGS: 4   **PREP TIME:** 10 MIN   **COOK TIME:** 25 MIN   **FREEZE-DRY TIME:** 24-48 HRS

Ingredients:

- 12 oz (340g) macaroni or pasta of your choice
- 2 cups (480ml) unsweetened non-dairy milk (such as almond milk or soy milk)
- 1 cup (120g) raw cashews, soaked in water for at least 4 hours or overnight
- 1/4 cup (30g) nutritional yeast
- 2 tablespoons lemon juice
- 2 tablespoons olive oil
- 2 cloves garlic, minced
- 1 teaspoon onion powder
- 1 teaspoon Dijon mustard
- 1/2 teaspoon turmeric powder (for color)
- Salt and pepper to taste
- **Fresh parsley for garnish (optional)**

Instructions:

1. Cook the pasta according to the package instructions until al dente. Drain and set aside.
2. In a blender, combine the soaked cashews, non-dairy milk, nutritional yeast, lemon juice, olive oil, minced garlic, onion powder, Dijon mustard, turmeric powder, salt, and pepper. Blend until smooth and creamy.
3. Pour the cashew "cheeze" sauce into a saucepan and heat over medium-low heat, stirring frequently, until warmed through.
4. Add the cooked macaroni or pasta to the saucepan with the "cheeze" sauce. Stir until the pasta is evenly coated with the sauce.
5. Cook for an additional 2-3 minutes, or until heated through.
6. Taste and adjust the seasoning with more salt and pepper if needed.
7. Remove from heat and garnish with fresh parsley, if desired.

For Freeze-Drying:

- **Prepare**: Allow the Vegan Mac N "Cheeze" to cool completely after cooking. Portion the dish into serving-sized portions.
- **Freeze**: Place the portions on freeze-drying trays, making sure they're not touching each other.
- **Freeze Dry**: Freeze dry the Vegan Mac N "Cheeze" at -40°F for 24 to 48 hours until completely dry.
- **Store**: Once dry, remove the freeze-dried dish from the trays and store them in airtight containers or vacuum-sealed bags.

Rehydrating:

- **Rehydrate**: To rehydrate the freeze-dried Vegan Mac N "Cheeze," place a portion in a bowl or dish. Add enough hot water to cover the dish completely. Let the dish soak in the hot water for about 10-15 minutes, stirring occasionally, until fully rehydrated and heated through.
- **Serve**: Drain any excess water, if necessary, and enjoy your rehydrated Vegan Mac N "Cheeze"!

Best Shakshuka

SERVINGS: 4   **PREP TIME:** 20 MIN   **COOK TIME:** 30 MIN   **FREEZE-DRY TIME:** 24-48 HRS

Ingredients:

2 tablespoons olive oil
1 onion, chopped
1 red bell pepper, chopped
3 cloves garlic, minced
1 teaspoon ground cumin
1 teaspoon paprika
1/2 teaspoon chili powder (optional for added heat)
1 can (28 oz) crushed tomatoes
4-6 large eggs
Salt and pepper to taste

Fresh parsley or cilantro for garnish
Crusty bread or pita for serving

Instructions:

1. Heat the olive oil in a large skillet over medium heat.
2. Add the chopped onion and red bell pepper to the skillet. Sauté until softened, about 5 minutes.
3. Add the minced garlic, ground cumin, paprika, and chili powder (if using) to the skillet. Cook for an additional 1-2 minutes until fragrant.
4. Pour the crushed tomatoes into the skillet and stir to combine. Bring the mixture to a simmer and let it cook for about 10-15 minutes, allowing the flavors to meld together and the sauce to thicken.
5. Using a spoon, create small wells in the tomato sauce for the eggs.
6. Crack the eggs, one at a time, into each well. Season the eggs with salt and pepper to taste.
7. Cover the skillet and let the shakshuka cook for about 5-8 minutes, or until the egg whites are set but the yolks are still runny.
8. Remove the skillet from heat and garnish the shakshuka with fresh parsley or cilantro.
9. Serve the shakshuka hot with crusty bread or pita for dipping.

For Freeze-Drying:

- **Prepare**: Allow the Best Shakshuka to cool completely after cooking. Portion the dish into serving-sized portions.
- **Freeze**: Place the portions on freeze-drying trays, making sure they're not touching each other.
- **Freeze Dry**: Freeze dry the Shakshuka at -40°F for 24 to 48 hours until completely dry.
- **Store**: Once dry, remove the freeze-dried dish from the trays and store them in airtight containers or vacuum-sealed bags.

Rehydrating:

- **Rehydrate**: To rehydrate the freeze-dried Shakshuka, place a portion in a bowl or dish. Add enough hot water to cover the dish completely. Let the dish soak in the hot water for about 10-15 minutes, stirring occasionally, until fully rehydrated and heated through.
- **Serve**: Drain any excess water, if necessary, and enjoy your rehydrated Best Shakshuka!

Sheet Pan Gnocchi

SERVINGS: 4   **PREP TIME:** 15 MIN   **COOK TIME:** 25 MIN   **FREEZE-DRY TIME:** 24-48 HRS

Ingredients:

1 lb (450g) store-bought or homemade gnocchi
2 tablespoons olive oil
2 cloves garlic, minced
1 pint (about 10 oz or 280g) cherry tomatoes, halved
1 bell pepper, chopped
1 small red onion, chopped
1 cup (150g) mushrooms, sliced
2 cups (60g) fresh spinach leaves
1/2 teaspoon dried basil
1/2 teaspoon dried oregano
Salt and pepper to taste
Grated Parmesan cheese for serving (optional)

Instructions:

1. Preheat your oven to 425°F.
2. In a large bowl, toss the gnocchi with olive oil and minced garlic until evenly coated.
3. Spread the gnocchi in a single layer on a baking sheet lined with parchment paper.
4. Arrange the cherry tomatoes, bell pepper, red onion, and mushrooms around the gnocchi on the baking sheet.
5. Sprinkle the dried basil, dried oregano, salt, and pepper over the gnocchi and vegetables.
6. Roast in the preheated oven for 20-25 minutes, stirring halfway through, until the gnocchi is golden and crispy and the vegetables are tender.
7. Remove from the oven and stir in the fresh spinach leaves until wilted.
8. Serve the sheet pan gnocchi hot, sprinkled with grated Parmesan cheese if desired.

For Freeze-Drying:

- **Prepare**: Allow the Sheet Pan Gnocchi to cool completely after cooking. Portion the dish into serving-sized portions.
- **Freeze**: Place the portions on freeze-drying trays, making sure they're not touching each other.
- **Freeze Dry**: Freeze dry the Sheet Pan Gnocchi at -40°F for 24 to 48 hours until completely dry.
- **Store**: Once dry, remove the freeze-dried dish from the trays and store them in airtight containers or vacuum-sealed bags.

Rehydrating:

- **Rehydrate**: To rehydrate the freeze-dried Sheet Pan Gnocchi, place a portion in a bowl or dish. Add enough hot water to cover the dish completely. Let the dish soak in the hot water for about 10-15 minutes, stirring occasionally, until fully rehydrated and heated through.
- **Serve**: Drain any excess water, if necessary, and enjoy your rehydrated Sheet Pan Gnocchi!

Spicy Mushroom Larb

SERVINGS: 4   **PREP TIME:** 15 MIN   **COOK TIME:** 25 MIN   **FREEZE-DRY TIME:** 24-48 HRS

Ingredients:

1 lb mushrooms, finely chopped (such as shiitake, cremini, or button)
2 tablespoons vegetable oil
2 shallots, finely chopped
3 cloves garlic, minced
1 tablespoon ginger, minced
2 Thai bird's eye chilies, finely chopped (adjust to taste)
3 tablespoons soy sauce
2 tablespoons lime juice
1 tablespoon brown sugar
1 teaspoon chili flakes (adjust to taste)
1/4 cup fresh cilantro, chopped

1/4 cup fresh mint leaves, chopped
Salt and pepper to taste
Lettuce leaves or rice for serving

Instructions:

1. Heat the vegetable oil in a large skillet over medium-high heat.
2. Add the finely chopped mushrooms to the skillet and cook, stirring occasionally, until they release their moisture and become golden brown and crispy, about 8-10 minutes.
3. Add the shallots, minced garlic, minced ginger, and chopped Thai bird's eye chilies to the skillet. Cook for an additional 2-3 minutes until fragrant.
4. In a small bowl, whisk together the soy sauce, lime juice, brown sugar, and chili flakes.
5. Pour the sauce mixture over the cooked mushrooms in the skillet. Stir to combine and coat the mushrooms evenly.
6. Cook for another 2-3 minutes, allowing the sauce to thicken and coat the mushrooms.
7. Remove the skillet from heat and stir in the chopped cilantro and mint leaves. Season with salt and pepper to taste.
8. Serve the spicy mushroom larb hot, spooned into lettuce leaves or over rice.

For Freeze-Drying:

- **Prepare**: Allow the Spicy Mushroom Larb to cool completely after cooking. Portion the dish into serving-sized portions.
- **Freeze**: Place the portions on freeze-drying trays, making sure they're not touching each other.
- **Freeze Dry**: Freeze dry the Spicy Mushroom Larb at -40°F for 24 to 48 hours until completely dry.
- **Store**: Once dry, remove the freeze-dried dish from the trays and store them in airtight containers or vacuum-sealed bags.

Rehydrating:

- **Rehydrate**: To rehydrate the freeze-dried Spicy Mushroom Larb, place a portion in a bowl or dish. Add enough hot water to cover the dish completely. Let the dish soak in the hot water for about 10-15 minutes, stirring occasionally, until fully rehydrated and heated through.
- **Serve**: Drain any excess water, if necessary, and enjoy your rehydrated Spicy Mushroom Larb!

Homemade Falafel

SERVINGS: 4   **PREP TIME:** 15 MIN   **COOK TIME:** 25 MIN   **FREEZE-DRY TIME:** 24-48 HRS

Ingredients:

- 1 cup dried chickpeas (not canned)
- 1/2 small onion, chopped
- 3 cloves garlic, minced
- 1/4 cup fresh parsley, chopped
- 1/4 cup fresh cilantro, chopped
- 1 teaspoon ground cumin
- 1 teaspoon ground coriander
- 1/2 teaspoon baking powder
- Salt and pepper to taste
- Vegetable oil for frying

Instructions:

1. Place the dried chickpeas in a large bowl and cover them with water. Let them soak overnight or for at least 8 hours.
2. After soaking, drain the chickpeas and transfer them to a food processor.
3. Add the chopped onion, minced garlic, fresh parsley, fresh cilantro, ground cumin, ground coriander, baking powder, salt, and pepper to the food processor.
4. Pulse the mixture until it forms a coarse paste, stopping to scrape down the sides of the bowl as needed. The mixture should be finely ground but not pureed.
5. Transfer the falafel mixture to a bowl, cover, and refrigerate for at least 1 hour to firm up.
6. After chilling, shape the falafel mixture into small balls or patties about 1.5 inches (3-4 cm) in diameter.
7. Heat vegetable oil in a deep skillet or pot to 350°F.
8. Carefully fry the falafel in batches until golden brown and crispy, about 3-4 minutes per side.
9. Remove the falafel from the oil using a slotted spoon and drain on paper towels.
10. Serve the falafel hot with tahini sauce, hummus, pita bread, and your favorite toppings.

For Freeze-Drying:

- **Prepare**: Allow the Homemade Falafel to cool completely after cooking.
- **Freeze**: Place the falafel balls or patties on freeze-drying trays, making sure they're not touching each other.
- **Freeze Dry**: Freeze dry the falafel at -40°F for 24 to 48 hours until completely dry.
- **Store**: Once dry, remove the freeze-dried falafel from the trays and store them in airtight containers or vacuum-sealed bags.

Rehydrating:

- **Rehydrate**: To rehydrate the freeze-dried falafel, place a portion in a bowl or dish. Add enough hot water to cover the falafel completely. Let the falafel soak in the hot water for about 10-15 minutes, stirring occasionally, until fully rehydrated and heated through.
- **Serve**: Drain any excess water, if necessary, and enjoy your rehydrated Homemade Falafel!

Chapter Four

Meat Lovers, These Are For You!

Stir-Fried Beef and Broccoli

SERVINGS: 4   **PREP TIME:** 15 MIN   **COOK TIME:** 15 MIN   **FREEZE-DRY TIME:** 24-48 HRS

Ingredients:

1 lb (450g) flank steak, thinly sliced against the grain
3 cups broccoli florets
2 tablespoons vegetable oil, divided
3 cloves garlic, minced
1 teaspoon fresh ginger, minced
1/4 cup soy sauce
2 tablespoons oyster sauce
1 tablespoon brown sugar
1 tablespoon cornstarch
1/4 cup water
Cooked rice or noodles for serving

Instructions:

1. In a small bowl, whisk together the soy sauce, oyster sauce, brown sugar, cornstarch, and water to make the sauce. Set aside.
2. Heat 1 tablespoon of vegetable oil in a large skillet or wok over high heat.
3. Add the thinly sliced flank steak to the skillet in a single layer and let it sear without stirring for about 1 minute.
4. Stir-fry the beef for another 1-2 minutes, or until browned and cooked through. Remove the beef from the skillet and set it aside.
5. In the same skillet, heat the remaining tablespoon of vegetable oil over medium-high heat.
6. Add the minced garlic and minced ginger to the skillet and stir-fry for about 30 seconds, or until fragrant.
7. Add the broccoli florets to the skillet and stir-fry for 2-3 minutes, or until crisp-tender.
8. Return the cooked beef to the skillet and pour the sauce over the beef and broccoli.
9. Stir well to coat the beef and broccoli evenly with the sauce.
10. Cook for another 1-2 minutes, or until the sauce has thickened and everything is heated through.
11. Serve the stir-fried beef and broccoli hot over cooked rice or noodles.

For Freeze-Drying:

- **Prepare:** Allow the Stir-Fried Beef and Broccoli to cool completely after cooking. Portion the dish into serving-sized portions.
- **Freeze:** Place the portions on freeze-drying trays, making sure they're not touching each other.
- **Freeze Dry:** Freeze dry the Stir-Fried Beef and Broccoli at -40°F for 24 to 48 hours until completely dry.
- **Store:** Once dry, remove the freeze-dried dish from the trays and store them in airtight containers or vacuum-sealed bags.

Rehydrating:

- **Rehydrate:** To rehydrate the freeze-dried Stir-Fried Beef and Broccoli, place a portion in a bowl or dish. Add enough hot water to cover the dish completely. Let the dish soak in the hot water for about 10-15 minutes, stirring occasionally, until fully rehydrated and heated through.
- **Serve:** Drain any excess water, if necessary, and enjoy your rehydrated Stir-Fried Beef and Broccoli!

Bacon Alfredo Pasta

SERVINGS: 4   **PREP TIME:** 15 MIN   **COOK TIME:** 20 MIN   **FREEZE-DRY TIME:** 24-48 HRS

Ingredients:

16 oz (450g) fettuccine or pasta of your choice
1/4 lb bacon, diced
1/4 cup butter
1/2 cup all-purpose flour
1.5 cups chicken broth
1 cup heavy whipping cream
1 cup grated Parmesan cheese
Parsley for garnish (optional)

Instructions:

1. Cook the fettuccine or pasta according to the package instructions until al dente. Drain and set aside.
2. In a large skillet, heat the olive oil over medium-high heat.
3. Add the diced bacon to the skillet and season with salt and pepper. Cook until browned and cooked through, about 5 minutes. Remove the bacon from the skillet and set aside.
4. In the same skillet, add the minced garlic and cook for about 1 minute, or until fragrant.
5. Reduce the heat to medium and pour in the heavy cream. Stir to combine with the garlic.
6. Add the grated Parmesan cheese to the skillet and stir until melted and the sauce is smooth and creamy.
7. Return the cooked bacon to the skillet and stir to coat with the Alfredo sauce.
8. Add the cooked fettuccine or pasta to the skillet and toss until evenly coated with the sauce.
9. Cook for an additional 2-3 minutes, or until heated through.
10. Taste and adjust the seasoning with more salt and pepper if needed.
11. Remove from heat and garnish with chopped fresh parsley, if desired.
12. Serve the Bacon Alfredo Pasta hot, sprinkled with more grated Parmesan cheese on top.

For Freeze-Drying:

- **Prepare**: Allow the Bacon Alfredo Pasta to cool completely after cooking. Portion the dish into serving-sized portions.
- **Freeze**: Place the portions on freeze-drying trays, making sure they're not touching each other.
- **Freeze Dry**: Freeze dry the Bacon Alfredo Pasta at -40°F for 24 to 48 hours until completely dry.
- **Store**: Once dry, remove the freeze-dried dish from the trays and store them in airtight containers or vacuum-sealed bags.

Rehydrating:

- **Rehydrate**: To rehydrate the freeze-dried Bacon Alfredo Pasta, place a portion in a bowl or dish. Add enough hot water to cover the dish completely. Let the dish soak in the hot water for about 10-15 minutes, stirring occasionally, until fully rehydrated and heated through.
- **Serve**: Drain any excess water, if necessary, and enjoy your rehydrated Bacon Alfredo Pasta!

Pork Chops with Apples and Onions

SERVINGS: 4   **PREP TIME:** 15 MIN   **COOK TIME:** 30 MIN   **FREEZE-DRY TIME:** 24-48 HRS

Ingredients:

4 bone-in pork chops
Salt and pepper to taste
2 tablespoons olive oil
2 apples, cored and sliced (use your favorite variety)
2 onions, thinly sliced
2 tablespoons brown sugar
1/2 cup (120ml) apple cider or apple juice
1/2 teaspoon ground cinnamon
1/4 teaspoon ground nutmeg
Fresh parsley, chopped, for garnish (optional)

Instructions:

1. Season both sides of the pork chops with salt and pepper.
2. Heat the olive oil in a large skillet over medium-high heat.
3. Add the pork chops to the skillet and cook for about 4-5 minutes per side, or until golden brown and cooked through. Remove the pork chops from the skillet and set aside.
4. In the same skillet, add the sliced apples and onions. Cook, stirring occasionally, until the apples and onions are softened and caramelized, about 5-7 minutes.
5. Sprinkle the brown sugar over the apples and onions and stir to combine.
6. Pour the apple cider or apple juice into the skillet and stir, scraping up any browned bits from the bottom of the skillet.
7. Add the ground cinnamon and ground nutmeg to the skillet and stir to combine.
8. Return the pork chops to the skillet, nestling them among the apples and onions.
9. Reduce the heat to medium-low, cover, and let everything simmer for another 5-10 minutes, allowing the flavors to meld together.
10. Taste and adjust the seasoning with more salt and pepper if needed.
11. Remove from heat and garnish with chopped fresh parsley, if desired.
12. Serve the Pork Chops with Apples and Onions hot, with the caramelized apples and onions spooned over the pork chops.

For Freeze-Drying:

- **Prepare**: Allow the Pork Chops with Apples and Onions to cool completely after cooking. Portion the dish into serving-sized portions.
- **Freeze**: Place the portions on freeze-drying trays, making sure they're not touching each other.
- **Freeze Dry**: Freeze dry the Pork Chops with Apples and Onions at -40°F for 24 to 48 hours until completely dry.
- **Store**: Once dry, remove the freeze-dried dish from the trays and store them in airtight containers or

Rehydrating:

- **Rehydrate**: To rehydrate the freeze-dried Pork Chops with Apples and Onions, place a portion in a bowl or dish. Add enough hot water to cover the dish completely. Let the dish soak in the hot water for about 10-15 minutes, stirring occasionally, until fully rehydrated and heated through.
- **Store**: Drain any excess water, if necessary, and enjoy your rehydrated Pork Chops with Apples and Onions!

Lamb Curry

SERVINGS: 4   **PREP TIME:** 20 MIN   **COOK TIME:** 1.5 HRS   **FREEZE-DRY TIME:** 24-48 HRS

Ingredients:

1 lb (450g) boneless lamb shoulder, cut into bite-sized pieces
2 tablespoons vegetable oil
1 large onion, chopped
3 cloves garlic, minced
1 tablespoon fresh ginger, minced
2 tablespoons curry powder
1 teaspoon ground cumin
1 teaspoon ground coriander
1/2 teaspoon ground turmeric
1/4 teaspoon cayenne pepper (adjust to taste)
1 can (14 oz) diced tomatoes
1 can (14 oz) coconut milk
Salt and pepper to taste
Fresh cilantro, chopped, for garnish (optional)
Cooked rice or naan bread for serving

Instructions:

1. Heat the vegetable oil in a large skillet or Dutch oven over medium-high heat.
2. Add the chopped onion to the skillet and cook until softened and translucent, about 5 minutes.
3. Add the minced garlic and minced ginger to the skillet and cook for another 1-2 minutes until fragrant.
4. Add the curry powder, ground cumin, ground coriander, ground turmeric, and cayenne pepper to the skillet. Stir to coat the onions and spices evenly.
5. Add the bite-sized pieces of lamb to the skillet and brown on all sides, about 5-7 minutes.
6. Once the lamb is browned, pour in the diced tomatoes and coconut milk. Stir to combine.
7. Bring the curry to a simmer, then reduce the heat to low and cover the skillet.
8. Let the curry simmer gently for about 1-1.5 hours, stirring occasionally, until the lamb is tender and the flavors have melded together.
9. Taste and adjust the seasoning with salt and pepper if needed.
10. Remove from heat and garnish with chopped fresh cilantro, if desired.
11. Serve the Lamb Curry hot, with cooked rice or naan bread on the side.

For Freeze-Drying:

- **Prepare**: Allow the Lamb Curry to cool completely after cooking. Portion the dish into serving-sized portions.
- **Freeze**: Place the portions on freeze-drying trays, making sure they're not touching each other.
- **Freeze Dry**: Freeze dry the Lamb Curry at -40°F for 24 to 48 hours until completely dry.
- **Store**: Once dry, remove the freeze-dried dish from the trays and store them in airtight containers or vacuum-sealed bags.

Rehydrating:

- **Rehydrate**: To rehydrate the freeze-dried Lamb Curry, place a portion in a bowl or dish. Add enough hot water to cover the dish completely. Let the dish soak in the hot water for about 10-15 minutes, stirring occasionally, until fully rehydrated and heated through.
- **Serve**: Drain any excess water, if necessary, and enjoy your rehydrated Lamb Curry!

Turkey Meatballs in Marinara Sauce

SERVINGS: 4   **PREP TIME:** 15 MIN   **COOK TIME:** 50 MIN   **FREEZE-DRY TIME:** 24-48 HRS

Ingredients:

For the meatballs:
1 lb (450g) ground turkey
1/2 cup breadcrumbs
1/4 cup grated Parmesan cheese
1 egg
2 cloves garlic, minced
2 tablespoons fresh parsley, chopped
1 teaspoon dried oregano
1/2 teaspoon salt
1/4 teaspoon black pepper

For the marinara sauce:
1 tablespoon olive oil
1 onion, finely chopped

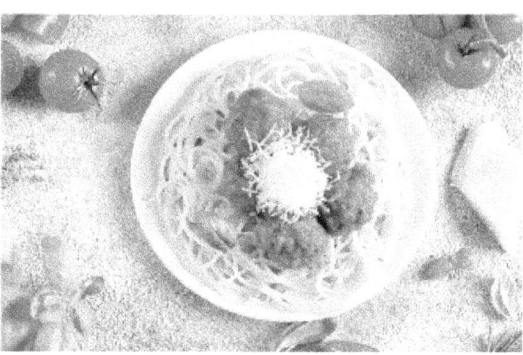

2 cloves garlic, minced
1 can (14 oz) crushed tomatoes
1 teaspoon dried basil
1 teaspoon dried oregano
Salt and pepper to taste

Instructions:

1. Preheat your oven to 400°F.
2. In a large bowl, combine the ground turkey, breadcrumbs, grated Parmesan cheese, egg, minced garlic, chopped parsley, dried oregano, salt, and black pepper. Mix until well combined.
3. Shape the turkey mixture into meatballs, about 1 to 1.5 inches (2.5 to 4 cm) in diameter, and place them on a baking sheet lined with parchment paper.
4. Bake the meatballs in the preheated oven for 15-20 minutes, or until cooked through and browned on the outside.
5. While the meatballs are baking, prepare the marinara sauce. Heat the olive oil in a large skillet over medium heat.
6. Add the finely chopped onion to the skillet and cook until softened, about 5 minutes.
7. Add the minced garlic to the skillet and cook for another 1-2 minutes until fragrant.
8. Pour the crushed tomatoes into the skillet and stir to combine with the onions and garlic.
9. Season the marinara sauce with dried basil, dried oregano, salt, and pepper to taste. Simmer for 10-15 minutes, stirring occasionally, to allow the flavors to meld together.
10. Once the meatballs are cooked, add them to the skillet with the marinara sauce. Gently stir to coat the meatballs with the sauce.
11. Simmer the meatballs in the marinara sauce for an additional 5-10 minutes to heat through.

For Freeze-Drying:

- **Prepare**: Allow the Turkey Meatballs in Marinara Sauce to cool completely after cooking. Portion the dish into serving-sized portions, making sure to include both meatballs and sauce.
- **Freeze**: Place the portions on freeze-drying trays, making sure they're not touching each other.
- **Freeze Dry**: Freeze dry the Turkey Meatballs in Marinara Sauce at -40°F for 24 to 48 hours until completely dry.
- **Store**: Once dry, remove the freeze-dried dish from the trays and store them in airtight containers or vacuum-sealed bags.

Rehydrating:

- **Rehydrate**: To rehydrate the freeze-dried Turkey Meatballs in Marinara Sauce, place a portion in a bowl or dish. Add enough hot water to cover the dish completely. Let the dish soak in the hot water for about 10-15 minutes, stirring occasionally, until fully rehydrated and heated through.
- **Serve**: Drain any excess water, if necessary, and enjoy your rehydrated Turkey Meatballs in Marinara Sauce!

Beef Tacos

SERVINGS: 4   **PREP TIME:** 20 MIN   **COOK TIME:** 25 MIN   **FREEZE-DRY TIME:** 24-48 HRS

Ingredients:

1 lb (450g) ground beef
1 tablespoon vegetable oil
1 small onion, diced
2 cloves garlic, minced
1 tablespoon chili powder
1 teaspoon ground cumin
1/2 teaspoon paprika
1/4 teaspoon dried oregano
Salt and pepper to taste
1/4 cup (60ml) tomato sauce
1/4 cup (60ml) beef broth or water
Taco shells or tortillas

Toppings of your choice: shredded lettuce, diced tomatoes, shredded cheese, sour cream, salsa, etc.

Instructions:

1. Heat the vegetable oil in a large skillet over medium heat.
2. Add the diced onion to the skillet and cook until softened, about 5 minutes.
3. Add the minced garlic to the skillet and cook for another 1-2 minutes until fragrant.
4. Add the ground beef to the skillet and cook, breaking it apart with a spoon, until browned and cooked through, about 5-7 minutes.
5. Drain any excess fat from the skillet, if necessary.
6. Stir in the chili powder, ground cumin, paprika, dried oregano, salt, and pepper, and cook for another 1-2 minutes until the spices are fragrant.
7. Pour in the tomato sauce and beef broth or water, and stir to combine.
8. Bring the mixture to a simmer and let it cook for another 5-10 minutes until the sauce thickens slightly.
9. Taste and adjust the seasoning with more salt and pepper if needed.
10. Remove from heat and assemble the tacos: Spoon the beef mixture into taco shells or tortillas and top with your favorite toppings.

For Freeze-Drying:

- **Prepare**: Allow the Beef Tacos to cool completely after cooking. Portion the taco filling into serving-sized portions.
- **Freeze**: Place the portions on freeze-drying trays, making sure they're not touching each other.
- **Freeze Dry**: Freeze dry the Beef Tacos at -40°F for 24 to 48 hours until completely dry.
- **Store**: Once dry, remove the freeze-dried taco filling from the trays and store them in airtight containers or vacuum-sealed bags.

Rehydrating:

- **Rehydrate**: To rehydrate the freeze-dried Beef Tacos, place a portion in a bowl or dish. Add enough hot water to cover the taco filling completely. Let the filling soak in the hot water for about 10-15 minutes, stirring occasionally, until fully rehydrated and heated through.
- **Serve**: Drain any excess water, if necessary, and assemble your tacos with the rehydrated filling and fresh toppings.

Honey Garlic Chicken Thighs

SERVINGS: 4   **PREP TIME:** 15 MIN   **COOK TIME:** 40 MIN   **FREEZE-DRY TIME:** 24-48 HRS

Ingredients:

4 bone-in, skin-on chicken thighs
Salt and pepper to taste
2 tablespoons olive oil
4 cloves garlic, minced
1/4 cup (60ml) soy sauce
1/4 cup (60ml) honey
1 tablespoon rice vinegar
1 teaspoon sesame oil
1 tablespoon cornstarch
2 tablespoons water

Sesame seeds and chopped green onions for garnish (optional)

Instructions:

1. Preheat your oven to 400°F.
2. Pat the chicken thighs dry with paper towels and season them with salt and pepper on both sides.
3. Heat the olive oil in an oven-proof skillet over medium-high heat.
4. Place the chicken thighs in the skillet, skin-side down, and cook for 5-6 minutes until golden brown and crispy.
5. Flip the chicken thighs and cook for another 2-3 minutes on the other side.
6. Meanwhile, in a small bowl, whisk together the minced garlic, soy sauce, honey, rice vinegar, and sesame oil to make the sauce.
7. Pour the sauce over the chicken thighs in the skillet, making sure they are coated evenly.
8. Transfer the skillet to the preheated oven and bake for 20-25 minutes until the chicken is cooked through and the sauce is thickened and bubbly.
9. In a small bowl, mix the cornstarch and water to create a slurry.
10. Remove the skillet from the oven and transfer the chicken thighs to a plate.
11. Return the skillet to the stovetop over medium heat and add the cornstarch slurry to the sauce.
12. Cook, stirring constantly, until the sauce thickens, about 1-2 minutes.
13. Return the chicken thighs to the skillet and coat them with the thickened sauce.
14. Garnish with sesame seeds and chopped green onions, if desired.
15. Serve the Honey Garlic Chicken Thighs hot, with rice or your favorite side dishes.

For Freeze-Drying:

- **Prepare**: Allow the Honey Garlic Chicken Thighs to cool completely after cooking. Portion the chicken thighs into serving-sized portions.
- **Freeze**: Place the portions on freeze-drying trays, making sure they're not touching each other.
- **Freeze Dry**: Freeze dry the chicken thighs at -40°F for 24 to 48 hours until completely dry.
- **Store**: Once dry, remove the freeze-dried chicken thighs from the trays and store them in airtight containers or vacuum-sealed bags.

Rehydrating:

- **Rehydrate**: To rehydrate the freeze-dried Honey Garlic Chicken Thighs, place a portion in a bowl or dish. Add enough hot water to cover the chicken thighs completely. Let the chicken thighs soak in the hot water for about 10-15 minutes, stirring occasionally, until fully rehydrated and heated through.
- **Serve**: Drain any excess water, if necessary, and enjoy your rehydrated Honey Garlic Chicken Thighs!

Salmon Filets

SERVINGS: 4   **PREP TIME:** 10 MIN   **COOK TIME:** 15 MIN   **FREEZE-DRY TIME:** 24-48 HRS

Ingredients:

4 salmon filets
Salt and pepper to taste
2 tablespoons olive oil
1/4 cup (60ml) dry white wine (optional)
1/4 cup (60ml) chicken broth
2 tablespoons lemon juice
2 tablespoons fresh dill, chopped
1/4 cup (60ml) heavy cream
Lemon slices and additional fresh dill for garnish (optional)

Instructions:

1. Season the salmon filets with salt and pepper on both sides.
2. Heat the olive oil in a large skillet over medium-high heat.
3. Place the salmon filets in the skillet, skin-side down, and cook for 4-5 minutes until the skin is crispy and golden brown.
4. Carefully flip the salmon filets over and cook for another 3-4 minutes until cooked through.
5. Transfer the cooked salmon filets to a plate and cover to keep warm.
6. In the same skillet, add the white wine (if using) and chicken broth. Bring to a simmer and cook for 2-3 minutes to reduce slightly.
7. Stir in the lemon juice and chopped dill.
8. Reduce the heat to low and stir in the heavy cream. Cook for another 1-2 minutes until the sauce thickens slightly.
9. Taste and adjust the seasoning with more salt and pepper if needed.
10. Return the salmon filets to the skillet and spoon the dill sauce over them.
11. Cook for another minute to heat through.
12. Garnish with lemon slices and additional fresh dill, if desired.
13. Serve the Salmon Filets with Dill Sauce hot, with your favorite side dishes.

For Freeze-Drying:

- **Prepare**: Allow the Salmon Filets with Dill Sauce to cool completely after cooking. Portion the salmon filets into serving-size portions.
- **Freeze**: Place the portions on freeze-drying trays, making sure they're not touching each other.
- **Freeze Dry**: Freeze dry the salmon filets at -40°F for 24 to 48 hours until completely dry.
- **Store**: Once dry, remove the freeze-dried salmon filets from the trays and store them in airtight containers or vacuum-sealed bags.

Rehydrating:

- **Rehydrate**: To rehydrate the freeze-dried Salmon Filets with Dill Sauce, place a portion in a bowl or dish. Add enough hot water to cover the salmon filets completely. Let the salmon filets soak in the hot water for about 10-15 minutes, stirring occasionally, until fully rehydrated and heated through.
- **Serve**: Drain any excess water, if necessary, and enjoy your rehydrated Salmon Filets with Dill Sauce!

Meatloaf

SERVINGS: 4   **PREP TIME:** 20 MIN   **COOK TIME:** 1 HR   **FREEZE-DRY TIME:** 24-48 HRS

Ingredients:

1 lb (450g) ground beef
1/2 cup breadcrumbs
1/4 cup milk
1 small onion, finely chopped
1/2 bell pepper, finely chopped
2 cloves garlic, minced
1 egg, beaten
2 tablespoons ketchup
1 tablespoon Worcestershire sauce
1 teaspoon dried thyme
1 teaspoon dried oregano
Salt and pepper to taste

For the glaze:

1/4 cup ketchup
1 tablespoon brown sugar
1 teaspoon Dijon mustard

Instructions:

1. Preheat your oven to 350°F.
2. In a large mixing bowl, combine the ground beef, breadcrumbs, milk, chopped onion, chopped bell pepper, minced garlic, beaten egg, ketchup, Worcestershire sauce, dried thyme, dried oregano, salt, and pepper. Mix until well combined.
3. Transfer the meatloaf mixture to a greased loaf pan, shaping it into a loaf shape.
4. In a small bowl, mix together the ingredients for the glaze: ketchup, brown sugar, and Dijon mustard. Spread the glaze evenly over the top of the meatloaf.
5. Bake the meatloaf in the preheated oven for 1 hour, or until cooked through and the internal temperature reaches 160°F.
6. Remove the meatloaf from the oven and let it rest for a few minutes before slicing.
7. Serve slices of meatloaf hot with your favorite sides, such as mashed potatoes and green beans.

For Freeze-Drying:

- **Prepare**: Allow the Meatloaf to cool completely after cooking. Slice the meatloaf into individual portions.
- **Freeze**: Place the portions on freeze-drying trays, making sure they're not touching each other.
- **Freeze Dry**: Freeze dry the Meatloaf at -40°F for 24 to 48 hours until completely dry.
- **Store**: Once dry, remove the freeze-dried meatloaf portions from the trays and store them in airtight containers or vacuum-sealed bags.

Rehydrating:

- **Rehydrate**: To rehydrate the freeze-dried Meatloaf, place a portion in a bowl or dish. Add enough hot water to cover the meatloaf completely. Let the meatloaf soak in the hot water for about 10-15 minutes, stirring occasionally, until fully rehydrated and heated through.
- **Serve**: Drain any excess water, if necessary, and enjoy your rehydrated Meatloaf!

Pork Belly Ramen

SERVINGS: 4   **PREP TIME:** 15 MIN   **COOK TIME:** 30 MIN   **FREEZE-DRY TIME:** 24-48 HRS

Ingredients:

1 lb (450g) pork belly, skin removed and cut into thin slices
Salt and pepper to taste
2 tablespoons vegetable oil
4 cloves garlic, minced
1 tablespoon fresh ginger, minced
6 cups (1.5 liters) chicken broth
2 tablespoons soy sauce
1 tablespoon mirin (Japanese sweet rice wine)
2 teaspoons sesame oil
4 servings of ramen noodles

Toppings of your choice: soft-boiled eggs, sliced green onions, nori (seaweed), bamboo shoots, corn kernels, spinach, etc.

Instructions:

1. Season the pork belly slices with salt and pepper on both sides.
2. Heat the vegetable oil in a large pot over medium-high heat.
3. Add the pork belly slices to the pot and cook until browned and crispy on both sides, about 3-4 minutes per side. Remove the pork belly from the pot and set aside.
4. In the same pot, add the minced garlic and minced ginger. Cook for 1-2 minutes until fragrant.
5. Pour the chicken broth into the pot and bring to a simmer.
6. Stir in the soy sauce, mirin, and sesame oil. Let the broth simmer for 10-15 minutes to allow the flavors to meld together.
7. Meanwhile, cook the ramen noodles according to the package instructions. Drain and set aside.
8. To assemble the ramen bowls, divide the cooked noodles among serving bowls.
9. Ladle the hot broth over the noodles, making sure to evenly distribute the pork belly slices among the bowls.
10. Add your desired toppings to the ramen bowls.
11. Serve the Pork Belly Ramen hot, garnished with additional sliced green onions and nori, if desired.

For Freeze-Drying:

- **Prepare**: Allow the Pork Belly Ramen to cool completely after cooking. Portion the ramen into serving-sized portions, including the noodles, broth, pork belly, and toppings.
- **Freeze**: Place the portions on freeze-drying trays, making sure they're not touching each other.
- **Freeze Dry**: Freeze dry the Pork Belly Ramen at -40°F for 24 to 48 hours until completely dry.
- **Store**: Once dry, remove the freeze-dried ramen portions from the trays and store them in airtight containers or vacuum-sealed bags.

Rehydrating:

- **Rehydrate**: To rehydrate the freeze-dried Pork Belly Ramen, place a portion in a bowl or dish. Add enough hot water to cover the ramen completely. Let the ramen soak in the hot water for about 10-15 minutes, stirring occasionally, until fully rehydrated and heated through.
- **Serve**: Drain any excess water, if necessary, and enjoy your rehydrated Pork Belly Ramen!

Chapter Five

I Sea Food & I Eat It

Grilled Salmon with Lemon-Butter Sauce

SERVINGS: 4   **PREP TIME:** 15 MIN   **COOK TIME:** 15 MIN   **FREEZE-DRY TIME:** 24-48 HRS

Ingredients:

4 salmon filets
Salt and pepper to taste
2 tablespoons olive oil
2 tablespoons unsalted butter
2 cloves garlic, minced
Zest of 1 lemon
Juice of 1 lemon
2 tablespoons chopped fresh parsley
Lemon slices for garnish (optional)

Instructions:

1. Preheat your grill to medium-high heat.
2. Season the salmon filets with salt and pepper on both sides.
3. Brush the grill grates with olive oil to prevent sticking.
4. Place the salmon filets on the preheated grill, skin-side down.
5. Grill the salmon for 4-5 minutes on each side, or until cooked to your desired level of doneness and grill marks appear.
6. While the salmon is grilling, prepare the lemon-butter sauce. In a small saucepan, melt the butter over medium heat.
7. Add the minced garlic to the melted butter and cook for 1-2 minutes until fragrant.
8. Stir in the lemon zest and lemon juice, and cook for another minute.
9. Remove the saucepan from heat and stir in the chopped fresh parsley.
10. Once the salmon is cooked, transfer it to a serving platter.
11. Drizzle the lemon-butter sauce over the grilled salmon filets.
12. Garnish with lemon slices and additional chopped parsley, if desired.
13. Serve the Grilled Salmon with Lemon-Butter Sauce hot, with your favorite side dishes.

For Freeze-Drying:

- **Prepare**: Allow the Grilled Salmon with Lemon-Butter Sauce to cool completely after cooking. Portion the salmon filets into serving-size portions.
- **Freeze**: Place the portions on freeze-drying trays, making sure they're not touching each other.
- **Freeze Dry**: Freeze dry the salmon filets at -40°F for 24 to 48 hours until completely dry.
- **Store**: Once dry, remove the freeze-dried salmon filets from the trays and store them in airtight containers or vacuum-sealed bags.

Rehydrating:

- **Rehydrate**: To rehydrate the freeze-dried Grilled Salmon with Lemon-Butter Sauce, place a portion in a bowl or dish. Add enough hot water to cover the salmon completely. Let the salmon soak in the hot water for about 10-15 minutes, stirring occasionally, until fully rehydrated and heated through.
- **Store**: Drain any excess water, if necessary, and enjoy your rehydrated Grilled Salmon with Lemon-Butter Sauce!

Fish Tacos with Cabbage Slaw

SERVINGS: 4   **PREP TIME:** 35 MIN   **COOK TIME:** 15 MIN   **FREEZE-DRY TIME:** 24-48 HRS

Ingredients:

For the Fish:
1 lb (450g) white fish filets (such as cod or tilapia)
Salt and pepper to taste
1 tablespoon olive oil
1 teaspoon chili powder
1 teaspoon ground cumin
1/2 teaspoon smoked paprika
Juice of 1 lime

For Serving:
8 small corn or flour tortillas
Sliced avocado
Sliced jalapeños
Lime wedges
Hot sauce (optional)

For the Cabbage Slaw:
2 cups shredded green cabbage
1/4 cup chopped fresh cilantro
2 tablespoons mayonnaise
1 tablespoon lime juice
Salt and pepper to taste

Instructions:

1. Season the fish filets with salt and pepper on both sides.
2. In a small bowl, mix together the olive oil, chili powder, ground cumin, smoked paprika, and lime juice to make a marinade.
3. Place the fish filets in a shallow dish and pour the marinade over them, making sure they are evenly coated. Let them marinate for 15-30 minutes.
4. While the fish is marinating, prepare the cabbage slaw. In a mixing bowl, combine the shredded green cabbage, chopped cilantro, mayonnaise, lime juice, salt, and pepper. Toss until well combined. Set aside.
5. Heat a grill or grill pan over medium-high heat. Once hot, grill the fish filets for 3-4 minutes on each side, or until cooked through and flaky.
6. Remove the fish from the grill and let it rest for a few minutes. Then, flake the fish into bite-sized pieces using a fork.
7. Warm the tortillas on the grill for about 30 seconds on each side.
8. To assemble the tacos, place some flaked fish onto each tortilla. Top with a spoonful of cabbage slaw, sliced avocado, sliced jalapeños, and a squeeze of lime juice.
9. Serve the Fish Tacos with Cabbage Slaw hot, with lime wedges and hot sauce on the side.

For Freeze-Drying:

- **Prepare**: Allow the Fish Tacos with Cabbage Slaw to cool completely after cooking. Portion the tacos into serving-sized portions, including the tortillas, fish, cabbage slaw, and toppings.
- **Freeze**: Place the portions on freeze-drying trays, making sure they're not touching each other.
- **Freeze Dry**: Freeze dry the Fish Tacos at -40°F for 24 to 48 hours until completely dry.
- **Store**: Once dry, remove the freeze-dried taco portions from the trays and store them in airtight containers or vacuum-sealed bags.

Rehydrating:

- **Rehydrate**: To rehydrate the freeze-dried Fish Tacos with Cabbage Slaw, place a portion in a bowl or dish. Add enough hot water to cover the tacos completely. Let the tacos soak in the hot water for about 10-15 minutes, stirring occasionally, until fully rehydrated and heated through.
- **Serve**: Drain any excess water, if necessary, and enjoy your rehydrated Fish Tacos with Cabbage Slaw!

Crab Cakes with Remoulade Sauce

SERVINGS: 4   **PREP TIME:** 35 MIN   **COOK TIME:** 15 MIN   **FREEZE-DRY TIME:** 24-48 HRS

Ingredients:

For the Crab Cakes:
1 lb (450g) lump crabmeat, picked over for shells
1/2 cup breadcrumbs
1/4 cup mayonnaise
2 tablespoons chopped fresh parsley
1 tablespoon Dijon mustard
1 teaspoon Worcestershire sauce
1 teaspoon Old Bay seasoning
1/2 teaspoon garlic powder
Salt and pepper to taste
1 egg, beaten
2 tablespoons olive oil

For the Remoulade Sauce:
1/2 cup mayonnaise
2 tablespoons chopped fresh parsley
1 tablespoon chopped green onions
1 tablespoon capers, chopped
1 tablespoon lemon juice
1 teaspoon Dijon mustard
1 teaspoon Worcestershire sauce
1/2 teaspoon paprika
Salt and pepper to taste

Instructions:

1. In a large mixing bowl, combine the lump crabmeat, breadcrumbs, mayonnaise, chopped parsley, Dijon mustard, Worcestershire sauce, Old Bay seasoning, garlic powder, salt, and pepper. Mix until well combined.
2. Gently fold in the beaten egg until the mixture holds together.
3. Divide the crab mixture into equal portions and shape each portion into a patty.
4. Heat the olive oil in a large skillet over medium heat.
5. Add the crab cakes to the skillet and cook for 4-5 minutes on each side, or until golden brown and heated through.

6. Meanwhile, prepare the remoulade sauce. In a small bowl, combine the mayonnaise, chopped parsley, chopped green onions, capers, lemon juice, Dijon mustard, Worcestershire sauce, paprika, salt, and pepper. Mix until well combined. Adjust seasoning to taste.
7. Serve the hot crab cakes with the remoulade sauce on the side.

For Freeze-Drying:

- **Prepare**: Allow the Crab Cakes with Remoulade Sauce to cool completely after cooking. Portion the crab cakes into serving-sized portions.
- **Freeze**: Place the portions on freeze-drying trays, making sure they're not touching each other.
- **Freeze Dry**: Freeze dry the crab cakes at -40°F for 24 to 48 hours until completely dry.
- **Store**: Once dry, remove the freeze-dried crab cake portions from the trays and store them in airtight containers or vacuum-sealed bags.

Rehydrating:

- **Rehydrate**: To rehydrate the freeze-dried Crab Cakes with Remoulade Sauce, place a portion in a bowl or dish. Add enough hot water to cover the crab cakes completely. Let the crab cakes soak in the hot water for about 10-15 minutes, stirring occasionally, until fully rehydrated and heated through.
- **Serve**: Drain any excess water, if necessary, and enjoy your rehydrated Crab Cakes with Remoulade Sauce!

Fish Pie

SERVINGS: 4   **PREP TIME:** 15 MIN   **COOK TIME:** 45 MIN   **FREEZE-DRY TIME:** 24-48 HRS

Ingredients:

1 lb (450g) mixed white fish filets (such as cod, haddock, and salmon), cut into chunks
1 onion, finely chopped
2 carrots, diced
1 cup frozen peas
2 tablespoons butter
2 tablespoons all-purpose flour
1 cup fish or vegetable broth
1/2 cup milk
2 tablespoons chopped fresh parsley
Salt and pepper to taste
Mashed potatoes, for topping

Instructions:

1. Preheat your oven to 375°F.
2. In a large skillet, melt the butter over medium heat.
3. Add the chopped onion and diced carrots to the skillet and cook for 5-7 minutes until softened.
4. Stir in the all-purpose flour and cook for another minute to form a roux.
5. Gradually pour in the fish or vegetable broth and milk, stirring constantly to prevent lumps from forming.
6. Bring the mixture to a simmer and cook for 2-3 minutes until thickened.
7. Add the chunks of fish and frozen peas to the skillet, stirring gently to combine.
8. Cook for another 5 minutes until the fish is cooked through and the peas are heated.
9. Stir in the chopped fresh parsley and season with salt and pepper to taste.
10. Transfer the fish mixture to a baking dish.
11. Spread the mashed potatoes evenly over the top of the fish mixture, creating a smooth layer.
12. Bake the Fish Pie in the preheated oven for 25-30 minutes until the mashed potatoes are golden brown and the filling is bubbling.
13. Remove from the oven and let it cool slightly before serving.

For Freeze-Drying:

- **Prepare**: Allow the Fish Pie to cool completely after cooking. Cut the pie into individual portions, if desired.
- **Freeze**: Place the portions on freeze-drying trays, making sure they're not touching each other.
- **Freeze Dry**: Freeze dry the Fish Pie at -40°F for 24 to 48 hours until completely dry.
- **Store**: Once dry, remove the freeze-dried pie portions from the trays and store them in airtight containers or vacuum-sealed bags.

Rehydrating:

- **Rehydrate**: To rehydrate the freeze-dried Fish Pie, place a portion in a bowl or dish. Add enough hot water to cover the pie completely. Let the pie soak in the hot water for about 10-15 minutes, stirring occasionally, until fully rehydrated and heated through.
- **Serve**: Drain any excess water, if necessary, and enjoy your rehydrated Fish Pie!

Fish Cakes

SERVINGS: 4   **PREP TIME:** 15 MIN   **COOK TIME:** 15 MIN   **FREEZE-DRY TIME:** 24-48 HRS

Ingredients:

1 lb (450g) white fish filets (such as cod, haddock, or tilapia), cooked and flaked
2 cups mashed potatoes
1/4 cup chopped fresh parsley
1/4 cup chopped green onions
2 tablespoons lemon juice
1 teaspoon Dijon mustard
Salt and pepper to taste
1/2 cup breadcrumbs
2 tablespoons olive oil

Instructions:

1. In a large mixing bowl, combine the flaked cooked fish, mashed potatoes, chopped parsley, chopped green onions, lemon juice, Dijon mustard, salt, and pepper. Mix until well combined.
2. Shape the fish mixture into patties, about 1/2-inch thick.
3. Place the breadcrumbs on a plate. Coat each fish cake in breadcrumbs, pressing gently to adhere.
4. Heat the olive oil in a large skillet over medium heat.
5. Add the fish cakes to the skillet and cook for 3-4 minutes on each side, or until golden brown and heated through.
6. Remove the fish cakes from the skillet and drain on paper towels to remove any excess oil.
7. Serve the Fish Cakes hot, with your favorite dipping sauce or side dishes.

For Freeze-Drying:

- **Prepare:** Allow the Fish Cakes to cool completely after cooking.
- **Freeze:** Place the fish cakes on freeze-drying trays, making sure they're not touching each other.
- **Freeze Dry:** Freeze dry the Fish Cakes at -40°F for 24 to 48 hours until completely dry.
- **Store:** Once dry, remove the freeze-dried fish cakes from the trays and store them in airtight containers or vacuum-sealed bags.

Rehydrating:

- **Rehydrate:** To rehydrate the freeze-dried Fish Cakes, place a portion in a bowl or dish. Add enough hot water to cover the fish cakes completely. Let the fish cakes soak in the hot water for about 10-15 minutes, stirring occasionally, until fully rehydrated and heated through.
- **Serve:** Drain any excess water, if necessary, and enjoy your rehydrated Fish Cakes!

Baked Salmon Filets

SERVINGS: 4   **PREP TIME:** 10 MIN   **COOK TIME:** 15 MIN   **FREEZE-DRY TIME:** 24-48 HRS

Ingredients:

4 salmon filets
Salt and pepper to taste
2 tablespoons olive oil
2 cloves garlic, minced
1 teaspoon dried thyme
1 teaspoon dried rosemary
1 teaspoon dried parsley
1 lemon, sliced
Fresh parsley for garnish (optional)

Instructions:

1. Preheat your oven to 375°F.
2. Place the salmon filets on a baking sheet lined with parchment paper.
3. Season the salmon filets with salt and pepper to taste.
4. In a small bowl, mix together the olive oil, minced garlic, dried thyme, dried rosemary, and dried parsley.
5. Drizzle the herb mixture over the salmon filets, spreading it evenly.
6. Place lemon slices on top of each salmon filet.
7. Bake the salmon filets in the preheated oven for 12-15 minutes, or until the salmon is cooked through and flakes easily with a fork.
8. Remove the salmon filets from the oven and let them rest for a few minutes.
9. Garnish with fresh parsley, if desired, before serving.

For Freeze-Drying:

- **Prepare**: Allow the Baked Salmon Filets to cool completely after cooking.
- **Freeze**: Place the salmon filets on freeze-drying trays, making sure they're not touching each other.
- **Freeze Dry**: Freeze dry the salmon filets at -40°F for 24 to 48 hours until completely dry.
- **Store**: Once dry, remove the freeze-dried salmon filets from the trays and store them in airtight containers or vacuum-sealed bags.

Rehydrating:

- **Rehydrate**: To rehydrate the freeze-dried Baked Salmon Filets, place a portion in a bowl or dish. Add enough hot water to cover the salmon filets completely. Let the salmon filets soak in the hot water for about 10-15 minutes, stirring occasionally, until fully rehydrated and heated through.
- **Serve**: Drain any excess water, if necessary, and enjoy your rehydrated Baked Salmon Filets!

Tuna Casserole

SERVINGS: 4   **PREP TIME:** 20 MIN   **COOK TIME:** 40 MIN   **FREEZE-DRY TIME:** 24-48 HRS

Ingredients:

8 oz (225g) egg noodles
2 cans (10.5 oz each) condensed cream of mushroom soup
1 cup milk
2 cans (5 oz each) tuna, drained
1 cup frozen peas
1 cup shredded cheddar cheese
1/2 cup breadcrumbs
2 tablespoons butter, melted
Salt and pepper to taste
Optional: 1/2 cup chopped onion, 1/2 cup sliced mushrooms

Instructions:

1. Preheat your oven to 375°F. Grease a 9x13-inch baking dish.
2. Cook the egg noodles according to the package instructions until al dente. Drain and set aside.
3. In a large mixing bowl, combine the condensed cream of mushroom soup and milk. Stir until well combined.
4. Add the cooked egg noodles, drained tuna, frozen peas, shredded cheddar cheese, and optional chopped onion and sliced mushrooms to the bowl. Season with salt and pepper to taste. Mix until everything is evenly coated.
5. Transfer the mixture to the prepared baking dish and spread it out evenly.
6. In a small bowl, combine the breadcrumbs and melted butter. Sprinkle the breadcrumb mixture evenly over the top of the casserole.
7. Cover the baking dish with aluminum foil and bake in the preheated oven for 25 minutes.
8. Remove the foil and bake for an additional 10-15 minutes, or until the casserole is hot and bubbly and the breadcrumbs are golden brown.
9. Remove from the oven and let it cool slightly before serving.

For Freeze-Drying:

- **Prepare**: Allow the Tuna Casserole to cool completely after cooking. Portion the casserole into serving-sized portions.
- **Freeze**: Place the portions on freeze-drying trays, making sure they're not touching each other.
- **Freeze Dry**: Freeze dry the Tuna Casserole at -40°F for 24 to 48 hours until completely dry.
- **Store**: Once dry, remove the freeze-dried casserole portions from the trays and store them in airtight containers or vacuum-sealed bags.

Rehydrating:

- **Rehydrate**: To rehydrate the freeze-dried Tuna Casserole, place a portion in a bowl or dish. Add enough hot water to cover the casserole completely. Let the casserole soak in the hot water for about 10-15 minutes, stirring occasionally, until fully rehydrated and heated through.
- **Serve**: Drain any excess water, if necessary, and enjoy your rehydrated Tuna Casserole!

Cod with Tomato and Herb Sauce

SERVINGS: 4   **PREP TIME:** 15 MIN   **COOK TIME:** 20 MIN   **FREEZE-DRY TIME:** 24-48 HRS

Ingredients:

4 cod filets (about 6 oz each)
Salt and pepper to taste
2 tablespoons olive oil
2 cloves garlic, minced
1 small onion, finely chopped
1 can (14 oz) diced tomatoes
2 tablespoons tomato paste
1 teaspoon dried oregano
1 teaspoon dried basil
1/2 teaspoon dried thyme
1/2 teaspoon red pepper flakes (optional)
Fresh parsley for garnish

Instructions:

1. Preheat your oven to 375°F.
2. Season the cod filets with salt and pepper on both sides.
3. In a large oven-safe skillet, heat the olive oil over medium heat.
4. Add the minced garlic and chopped onion to the skillet and sauté for 2-3 minutes until softened and fragrant.
5. Stir in the diced tomatoes, tomato paste, dried oregano, dried basil, dried thyme, and red pepper flakes (if using). Cook for another 5 minutes, stirring occasionally, until the sauce thickens slightly.
6. Nestle the seasoned cod filets into the sauce in the skillet.
7. Transfer the skillet to the preheated oven and bake for 12-15 minutes, or until the cod is cooked through and flakes easily with a fork.
8. Remove from the oven and let it cool slightly before serving.
9. Garnish with fresh parsley before serving.

For Freeze-Drying:

- **Prepare**: Allow the Cod with Tomato and Herb Sauce to cool completely after cooking. Portion the cod filets with the tomato and herb sauce into serving-sized portions.
- **Freeze**: Place the portions on freeze-drying trays, making sure they're not touching each other.
- **Freeze Dry**: Freeze dry the Cod with Tomato and Herb Sauce at -40°F for 24 to 48 hours until completely dry.
- **Store**: Once dry, remove the freeze-dried portions from the trays and store them in airtight containers or vacuum-sealed bags.

Rehydrating:

- **Rehydrate**: To rehydrate the freeze-dried Cod with Tomato and Herb Sauce, place a portion in a bowl or dish. Add enough hot water to cover the cod and sauce completely. Let the cod and sauce soak in the hot water for about 10-15 minutes, stirring occasionally, until fully rehydrated and heated through.
- **Serve**: Drain any excess water, if necessary, and enjoy your rehydrated Cod with Tomato and Herb Sauce!

Seafood Chowder

SERVINGS: 4   **PREP TIME:** 15 MIN   **COOK TIME:** 35 MIN   **FREEZE-DRY TIME:** 24-48 HRS

Ingredients:

1 tablespoon butter
1 onion, chopped
2 cloves garlic, minced
2 stalks celery, chopped
2 carrots, diced
2 potatoes, peeled and diced
4 cups seafood or vegetable broth
1 cup frozen corn kernels
1 cup frozen peas
1 lb mixed seafood (such as shrimp, scallops, and white fish), cut into bite-sized pieces

1 cup heavy cream
Salt and pepper to taste
Chopped fresh parsley for garnish

Instructions:

1. In a large pot or Dutch oven, melt the butter over medium heat.
2. Add the chopped onion, minced garlic, chopped celery, and diced carrots to the pot. Cook for 5-7 minutes until the vegetables are softened.
3. Stir in the diced potatoes and seafood or vegetable broth. Bring the mixture to a boil, then reduce the heat to low and simmer for 10-15 minutes until the potatoes are tender.
4. Add the frozen corn kernels, frozen peas, and mixed seafood to the pot. Simmer for another 5-7 minutes until the seafood is cooked through.
5. Stir in the heavy cream and season the chowder with salt and pepper to taste. Cook for another 2-3 minutes until heated through.
6. Remove the pot from the heat and ladle the seafood chowder into bowls.
7. Garnish with chopped fresh parsley before serving.

For Freeze-Drying:

- **Prepare**: Allow the Seafood Chowder to cool completely after cooking. Portion the chowder into serving-sized portions.
- **Freeze**: Place the portions on freeze-drying trays, making sure they're not touching each other.
- **Freeze Dry**: Freeze dry the Seafood Chowder at -40°F for 24 to 48 hours until completely dry.
- **Store**: Once dry, remove the freeze-dried chowder portions from the trays and store them in airtight containers or vacuum-sealed bags.

Rehydrating:

- **Rehydrate**: To rehydrate the freeze-dried Seafood Chowder, place a portion in a pot or saucepan. Add enough hot water to cover the chowder completely. Heat the chowder over medium heat, stirring occasionally, until fully rehydrated and heated through.
- **Serve**: Adjust the seasoning if necessary and enjoy your rehydrated Seafood Chowder!

Shrimp Fried Rice

SERVINGS: 4   **PREP TIME:** 15 MIN   **COOK TIME:** 25 MIN   **FREEZE-DRY TIME:** 24-48 HRS

Ingredients:

2 cups cooked rice (preferably day-old)
1 lb shrimp, peeled and deveined
2 tablespoons soy sauce
1 tablespoon oyster sauce
1 tablespoon sesame oil
2 eggs, beaten
2 cloves garlic, minced
1 small onion, chopped
1 cup mixed vegetables (such as peas, carrots, and corn)
Salt and pepper to taste
Chopped green onions for garnish

Instructions:

1. In a small bowl, marinate the shrimp with soy sauce, oyster sauce, and sesame oil. Let it sit for 10-15 minutes.
2. Heat a large skillet or wok over medium-high heat. Add a tablespoon of oil.
3. Add the beaten eggs to the skillet and scramble until cooked through. Remove from the skillet and set aside.
4. In the same skillet, add another tablespoon of oil. Add the minced garlic and chopped onion. Cook until fragrant and onions are translucent.
5. Add the marinated shrimp to the skillet. Cook until shrimp are pink and cooked through, about 2-3 minutes.
6. Add the mixed vegetables to the skillet. Cook until vegetables are tender, about 3-4 minutes.
7. Add the cooked rice to the skillet. Stir-fry until everything is well combined and heated through.
8. Season with salt and pepper to taste.
9. Return the scrambled eggs to the skillet. Stir-fry for another minute.
10. Garnish with chopped green onions before serving.

For Freeze-Drying:

- **Prepare**: Allow the Shrimp Fried Rice to cool completely after cooking. Portion the fried rice into serving-sized portions.
- **Freeze**: Place the portions on freeze-drying trays, making sure they're not touching each other.
- **Freeze Dry**: Freeze dry the Shrimp Fried Rice at -40°F for 24 to 48 hours until completely dry.
- **Store**: Once dry, remove the freeze-dried portions from the trays and store them in airtight containers or vacuum-sealed bags.

Rehydrating:

- **Rehydrate**: To rehydrate the freeze-dried Shrimp Fried Rice, place a portion in a bowl or dish. Add enough hot water to cover the fried rice completely. Let the fried rice soak in the hot water for about 10-15 minutes, stirring occasionally, until fully rehydrated and heated through.
- **Serve**: Drain any excess water, if necessary, and enjoy your rehydrated Shrimp Fried Rice!

Chapter Six

Poultry Dishes You Must Make

Chicken Casserole

SERVINGS: 4 **PREP TIME:** 25 MIN **COOK TIME:** 30 MIN **FREEZE-DRY TIME:** 24-48 HRS

Ingredients:

2 cups cooked chicken, shredded or diced
2 cups cooked pasta (such as macaroni or penne)
1 cup frozen mixed vegetables (such as peas, carrots, and corn)
1 can (10.5 oz) condensed cream of chicken soup
1/2 cup milk
1 cup shredded cheddar cheese
Salt and pepper to taste
1/2 cup breadcrumbs
2 tablespoons butter, melted

Optional: chopped fresh parsley for garnish

Instructions:

1. Preheat your oven to 375°F. Grease a 9x13-inch baking dish.
2. In a large mixing bowl, combine the cooked chicken, cooked pasta, and frozen mixed vegetables.
3. In a separate bowl, mix together the condensed cream of chicken soup and milk until well combined.
4. Pour the soup mixture over the chicken, pasta, and vegetables in the mixing bowl. Add the shredded cheddar cheese and season with salt and pepper to taste. Mix until everything is evenly coated.
5. Transfer the mixture to the prepared baking dish and spread it out evenly.
6. In a small bowl, combine the breadcrumbs and melted butter. Sprinkle the breadcrumb mixture evenly over the top of the casserole.
7. Bake the Chicken Casserole in the preheated oven for 25-30 minutes until bubbly and golden brown on top.
8. Remove from the oven and let it cool slightly before serving.
9. Garnish with chopped fresh parsley, if desired, before serving.

For Freeze-Drying:

- **Prepare**: Allow the Chicken Casserole to cool completely after cooking. Portion the casserole into serving-sized portions.
- **Freeze**: Place the portions on freeze-drying trays, making sure they're not touching each other.
- **Freeze Dry**: Freeze dry the Chicken Casserole at -40°F for 24 to 48 hours until completely dry.
- **Store**: Once dry, remove the freeze-dried portions from the trays and store them in airtight containers or vacuum-sealed bags.

Rehydrating:

- **Rehydrate**: To rehydrate the freeze-dried Chicken Casserole, place a portion in a bowl or dish. Add enough hot water to cover the casserole completely. Let the casserole soak in the hot water for about 10-15 minutes, stirring occasionally, until fully rehydrated and heated through.
- **Serve**: Drain any excess water, if necessary, and enjoy your rehydrated Chicken Casserole!

Buffalo Chicken Wraps

SERVINGS: 4   **PREP TIME:** 20 MIN   **COOK TIME:** 5 MIN   **FREEZE-DRY TIME:** 24-48 HRS

Ingredients:

2 cups cooked chicken, shredded or diced
1/2 cup buffalo sauce (adjust to taste)
1/4 cup ranch or blue cheese dressing
4 large flour tortillas
1 cup shredded lettuce
1/2 cup diced tomatoes
1/4 cup diced red onion
1/4 cup crumbled blue cheese (optional)
Fresh cilantro or parsley for garnish (optional)

Instructions:

1. In a mixing bowl, combine the cooked chicken with buffalo sauce until well coated.
2. Warm the flour tortillas in a dry skillet or microwave for a few seconds to make them pliable.
3. Spread a tablespoon of ranch or blue cheese dressing onto each tortilla.
4. Divide the buffalo chicken mixture evenly among the tortillas, spreading it out into a line down the center.
5. Top the chicken with shredded lettuce, diced tomatoes, diced red onion, and crumbled blue cheese (if using).
6. Fold the sides of the tortillas over the filling, then roll them up tightly into wraps.
7. Optional: Grill the wraps on a skillet or grill pan for a few minutes on each side until golden brown and crispy.
8. Garnish with fresh cilantro or parsley, if desired, before serving.

For Freeze-Drying:

- **Prepare**: Allow the Buffalo Chicken Wraps to cool completely after assembling. Wrap each wrap tightly in plastic wrap or aluminum foil.
- **Freeze**: Place the wrapped wraps on freeze-drying trays, making sure they're not touching each other.
- **Freeze Dry**: Freeze dry the Buffalo Chicken Wraps at -40°F for 24 to 48 hours until completely dry.
- **Store**: Once dry, remove the freeze-dried wraps from the trays and store them in airtight containers or vacuum-sealed bags.

Rehydrating:

- **Rehydrate**: To rehydrate the freeze-dried Buffalo Chicken Wraps, remove them from the packaging and place them on a microwave-safe plate. Microwave each wrap on high for 1-2 minutes until heated through. Alternatively, you can rehydrate the wraps by placing them in a covered skillet with a splash of water over low heat until heated through.
- **Serve**: Once heated, let the wraps cool slightly before unwrapping and enjoying!

Chicken Alfredo Pasta

SERVINGS: 4   **PREP TIME:** 15 MIN   **COOK TIME:** 20 MIN   **FREEZE-DRY TIME:** 24-48 HRS

Ingredients:

8 oz (225g) fettuccine or pasta of your choice
2 boneless, skinless chicken breasts, sliced into thin strips
2 tablespoons olive oil
3 cloves garlic, minced
1 cup (240ml) heavy cream
1/2 cup (50g) grated Parmesan cheese, plus more for serving
Salt and pepper to taste
Fresh parsley, chopped, for garnish (optional)

Instructions:

1. Cook the fettuccine or pasta according to the package instructions until al dente. Drain and set aside.
2. In a large skillet, heat the olive oil over medium-high heat.
3. Add the sliced chicken breast to the skillet and season with salt and pepper. Cook until browned and cooked through, about 5-7 minutes per side. Remove the chicken from the skillet and set aside.
4. In the same skillet, add the minced garlic and cook for about 1 minute, or until fragrant.
5. Reduce the heat to medium and pour in the heavy cream. Stir to combine with the garlic.
6. Add the grated Parmesan cheese to the skillet and stir until melted and the sauce is smooth and creamy.
7. Return the cooked chicken to the skillet and stir to coat with the Alfredo sauce.
8. Add the cooked fettuccine or pasta to the skillet and toss until evenly coated with the sauce.
9. Cook for an additional 2-3 minutes, or until heated through.
10. Taste and adjust the seasoning with more salt and pepper if needed.
11. Remove from heat and garnish with chopped fresh parsley, if desired.
12. Serve the Chicken Alfredo Pasta hot, sprinkled with more grated Parmesan cheese on top.

For Freeze-Drying:

- **Prepare:** Allow the Chicken Alfredo Pasta to cool completely after cooking. Portion the dish into serving-sized portions.
- **Freeze:** Place the portions on freeze-drying trays, making sure they're not touching each other.
- **Freeze Dry:** Freeze dry the Chicken Alfredo Pasta at -40°F for 24 to 48 hours until completely dry.
- **Store:** Once dry, remove the freeze-dried dish from the trays and store them in airtight containers or vacuum-sealed bags.

Rehydrating:

- **Rehydrate:** To rehydrate the freeze-dried Chicken Alfredo Pasta, place a portion in a bowl or dish. Add enough hot water to cover the dish completely. Let the dish soak in the hot water for about 10-15 minutes, stirring occasionally, until fully rehydrated and heated through.
- **Serve:** Drain any excess water, if necessary, and enjoy your rehydrated Chicken Alfredo Pasta!

Chicken Pot Pie

SERVINGS: 4   **PREP TIME:** 15 MIN   **COOK TIME:** 20 MIN   **FREEZE-DRY TIME:** 24-48 HRS

Ingredients:

1 pie crust (store-bought or homemade)
2 tablespoons butter
1 onion, chopped
2 carrots, diced
2 celery stalks, diced
2 cloves garlic, minced
1/4 cup all-purpose flour
2 cups chicken broth
1 cup milk
2 cups cooked chicken, shredded or diced
1 cup frozen peas
Salt and pepper to taste
1 egg, beaten (for egg wash)

Instructions:

1. Preheat your oven to 375°F.
2. In a large skillet, melt the butter over medium heat. Add the chopped onion, diced carrots, and diced celery. Cook until the vegetables are softened, about 5-7 minutes.
3. Add the minced garlic to the skillet and cook for an additional minute until fragrant.
4. Sprinkle the flour over the vegetables in the skillet. Stir to combine and cook for 1-2 minutes to remove the raw flour taste.
5. Gradually whisk in the chicken broth and milk until smooth. Bring the mixture to a simmer and cook until thickened, stirring occasionally, about 5 minutes.
6. Stir in the cooked chicken and frozen peas. Season with salt and pepper to taste. Remove from heat.
7. Roll out the pie crust and line a 9-inch pie dish with the bottom crust. Pour the chicken mixture into the pie dish.
8. Place the top crust over the filling and crimp the edges to seal. Cut a few slits in the top crust to allow steam to escape.
9. Brush the top crust with the beaten egg for a golden finish.
10. Bake the Chicken Pot Pie in the preheated oven for 35-40 minutes, or until the crust is golden brown and the filling is bubbly.
11. Remove from the oven and let it cool for a few minutes before serving.

For Freeze-Drying:

- **Prepare**: Allow the Chicken Pot Pie to cool completely after baking. Cut the pie into individual servings.
- **Freeze**: Place the servings on freeze-drying trays, making sure they're not touching each other.
- **Freeze Dry**: Freeze dry the Chicken Pot Pie at -40°F for 24 to 48 hours until completely dry.
- **Store**: Once dry, remove the freeze-dried servings from the trays and store them in airtight containers or vacuum-sealed bags.

Rehydrating:

- **Rehydrate**: To rehydrate the freeze-dried Chicken Pot Pie, place a serving in a bowl or dish. Add enough hot water to cover the pie completely. Let the pie soak in the hot water for about 10-15 minutes, stirring occasionally, until fully rehydrated and heated through.
- **Serve**: Drain any excess water, if necessary, and enjoy your rehydrated Chicken Pot Pie!

Chicken Enchiladas

SERVINGS: 4   **PREP TIME:** 20 MIN   **COOK TIME:** 25 MIN   **FREEZE-DRY TIME:** 24-48 HRS

Ingredients:

2 cups cooked chicken, shredded
1 cup enchilada sauce (store-bought or homemade)
1 cup shredded cheese (such as cheddar or Monterey Jack)
1/2 cup diced onion
1/2 cup diced bell pepper (any color)
1/2 cup canned black beans, drained and rinsed
1/2 cup canned corn kernels, drained
1/4 cup chopped fresh cilantro
8 small flour tortillas

Optional toppings: sliced green onions, diced tomatoes, sour cream, avocado slices

Instructions:

1. Preheat your oven to 375°F. Grease a 9x13-inch baking dish.
2. In a large mixing bowl, combine the shredded chicken, enchilada sauce, shredded cheese, diced onion, diced bell pepper, black beans, corn kernels, and chopped cilantro. Mix until everything is well combined.
3. Place a spoonful of the chicken mixture onto the center of each flour tortilla. Roll up the tortillas tightly and place them seam side down in the prepared baking dish.
4. Repeat with the remaining tortillas and chicken mixture, arranging them snugly in the baking dish.
5. Pour any remaining enchilada sauce over the top of the rolled tortillas in the baking dish.
6. Sprinkle additional shredded cheese on top, if desired.
7. Cover the baking dish with aluminum foil and bake in the preheated oven for 20-25 minutes, or until the enchiladas are heated through and the cheese is melted and bubbly.
8. Remove from the oven and let it cool slightly before serving.
9. Garnish with sliced green onions, diced tomatoes, sour cream, and avocado slices, if desired, before serving.

For Freeze-Drying:

- **Prepare**: Allow the Chicken Enchiladas to cool completely after baking. Cut the enchiladas into individual servings.
- **Freeze**: Place the servings on freeze-drying trays, making sure they're not touching each other.
- **Freeze Dry**: Freeze dry the Chicken Enchiladas at -40°F for 24 to 48 hours until completely dry.
- **Store**: Once dry, remove the freeze-dried servings from the trays and store them in airtight containers or vacuum-sealed bags.

Rehydrating:

- **Rehydrate**: To rehydrate the freeze-dried Chicken Enchiladas, place a serving in a bowl or dish. Add enough hot water to cover the enchiladas completely. Let the enchiladas soak in the hot water for about 10-15 minutes, stirring occasionally, until fully rehydrated and heated through.
- **Serve**: Drain any excess water, if necessary, and enjoy your rehydrated Chicken Enchiladas!

Chicken Curry

SERVINGS: 4   **PREP TIME:** 20 MIN   **COOK TIME:** 40 MIN   **FREEZE-DRY TIME:** 24-48 HRS

Ingredients:

- 1 lb boneless, skinless chicken thighs or breasts, cut into bite-sized pieces
- 2 tablespoons vegetable oil
- 1 onion, finely chopped
- 3 cloves garlic, minced
- 1 tablespoon fresh ginger, grated
- 2 tablespoons curry powder
- 1 teaspoon ground turmeric
- 1 teaspoon ground cumin
- 1 teaspoon ground coriander
- 1/2 teaspoon chili powder (adjust to taste)
- 1 can (14 oz) coconut milk
- 1 cup chicken broth
- 2 medium potatoes, peeled and diced
- 1 carrot, peeled and diced
- Salt and pepper to taste
- Fresh cilantro for garnish
- Cooked rice or naan bread, for serving

Instructions:

1. Heat vegetable oil in a large skillet or pot over medium heat. Add the chopped onion and cook until softened, about 5 minutes.
2. Add minced garlic and grated ginger to the skillet. Cook for another minute until fragrant.
3. Add the chicken pieces to the skillet and cook until browned on all sides, about 5-7 minutes.
4. Stir in the curry powder, ground turmeric, ground cumin, ground coriander, and chili powder. Cook for 1-2 minutes until the spices are fragrant.
5. Pour in the coconut milk and chicken broth. Bring the mixture to a simmer.
6. Add the diced potatoes and carrots to the skillet. Cover and simmer for 20-25 minutes until the chicken is cooked through and the vegetables are tender.
7. Season the chicken curry with salt and pepper to taste.
8. Garnish with fresh cilantro before serving.
9. Serve the chicken curry hot with cooked rice or naan bread.

For Freeze-Drying:

- **Prepare**: Allow the Chicken Curry to cool completely after cooking. Portion the curry into serving-sized portions.
- **Freeze**: Place the portions on freeze-drying trays, making sure they're not touching each other.
- **Freeze Dry**: Freeze dry the Chicken Curry at -40°F for 24 to 48 hours until completely dry.
- **Store**: Once dry, remove the freeze-dried portions from the trays and store them in airtight containers or vacuum-sealed bags.

Rehydrating:

- **Rehydrate**: To rehydrate the freeze-dried Chicken Curry, place a portion in a bowl or dish. Add enough hot water to cover the curry completely. Let the curry soak in the hot water for about 10-15 minutes, stirring occasionally, until fully rehydrated and heated through.
- **Serve**: Drain any excess water, if necessary, and enjoy your rehydrated Chicken Curry!

Chicken Parmesan

SERVINGS: 4   **PREP TIME:** 15 MIN   **COOK TIME:** 45 MIN   **FREEZE-DRY TIME:** 24-48 HRS

Ingredients:

4 boneless, skinless chicken breasts
Salt and pepper to taste
1 cup all-purpose flour
2 large eggs, beaten
1 cup breadcrumbs (Italian seasoned breadcrumbs work well)
1/2 cup grated Parmesan cheese
2 cups marinara sauce
1 cup shredded mozzarella cheese
Fresh basil leaves for garnish

Cooked spaghetti or pasta of your choice, for serving

Instructions:

1. Preheat your oven to 400°F.
2. Place the chicken breasts between two sheets of plastic wrap or parchment paper. Use a meat mallet or rolling pin to pound them to an even thickness of about 1/2 inch. Season both sides of the chicken breasts with salt and pepper.
3. Set up a breading station with three shallow dishes: one with flour, one with beaten eggs, and one with a mixture of breadcrumbs and grated Parmesan cheese.
4. Dredge each chicken breast in the flour, shaking off any excess. Dip it into the beaten eggs, allowing any excess to drip off. Then coat it evenly with the breadcrumb mixture, pressing gently to adhere.
5. Place the breaded chicken breasts on a baking sheet lined with parchment paper or aluminum foil. Bake in the preheated oven for 20-25 minutes, or until the chicken is cooked through and the crust is golden brown and crispy.
6. Remove the chicken from the oven and spoon marinara sauce over each breast, covering them evenly. Sprinkle shredded mozzarella cheese over the sauce.
7. Return the chicken to the oven and bake for an additional 5-10 minutes, or until the cheese is melted and bubbly.
8. Remove from the oven and let the Chicken Parmesan rest for a few minutes before serving.
9. Garnish with fresh basil leaves and serve with cooked spaghetti or pasta of your choice.

For Freeze-Drying:

- **Prepare**: Allow the Chicken Parmesan to cool completely after cooking. Cut the chicken breasts into individual servings.
- **Freeze**: Place the servings on freeze-drying trays, making sure they're not touching each other.
- **Freeze Dry**: Freeze dry the Chicken Parmesan at -40°F for 24 to 48 hours until completely dry.
- **Store**: Once dry, remove the freeze-dried servings from the trays and store them in airtight containers or vacuum-sealed bags.

Rehydrating:

- **Rehydrate**: To rehydrate the freeze-dried Chicken Parmesan, place a serving in a bowl or dish. Add enough hot water to cover the chicken completely. Let the chicken soak in the hot water for about 10-15 minutes, stirring occasionally, until fully rehydrated and heated through.
- **Serve**: Drain any excess water, if necessary, and enjoy your rehydrated Chicken Parmesan!

Chicken and Rice Soup

SERVINGS: 4   **PREP TIME:** 20 MIN   **COOK TIME:** 25 MIN   **FREEZE-DRY TIME:** 24-48 HRS

Ingredients:

- 1 tablespoon olive oil
- 1 onion, chopped
- 2 carrots, diced
- 2 celery stalks, diced
- 2 cloves garlic, minced
- 6 cups chicken broth
- 1 cup cooked chicken, shredded or diced
- 1 cup cooked rice
- 1 teaspoon dried thyme
- Salt and pepper to taste
- Fresh parsley for garnish

Instructions:

1. Heat olive oil in a large pot over medium heat. Add chopped onion, diced carrots, and diced celery. Cook until vegetables are softened, about 5-7 minutes.
2. Add minced garlic to the pot and cook for an additional minute until fragrant.
3. Pour in chicken broth and bring to a simmer.
4. Add shredded or diced cooked chicken, cooked rice, and dried thyme to the pot. Season with salt and pepper to taste.
5. Simmer the soup for 15-20 minutes to allow the flavors to meld together.
6. Taste and adjust seasoning if necessary.
7. Serve the Chicken and Rice Soup hot, garnished with fresh parsley.

For Freeze-Drying:

- **Prepare**: Allow the Chicken and Rice Soup to cool completely after cooking. Portion the soup into individual servings.
- **Freeze**: Place the servings on freeze-drying trays, making sure they're not touching each other.
- **Freeze Dry**: Freeze dry the Chicken and Rice Soup at -40°F for 24 to 48 hours until completely dry.
- **Store**: Once dry, remove the freeze-dried servings from the trays and store them in airtight containers or vacuum-sealed bags.

Rehydrating:

- **Rehydrate**: To rehydrate the freeze-dried Chicken and Rice Soup, place a serving in a bowl or dish. Add enough hot water to cover the soup completely. Let the soup soak in the hot water for about 10-15 minutes, stirring occasionally, until fully rehydrated and heated through.
- **Serve**: Drain any excess water, if necessary, and enjoy your rehydrated Chicken and Rice Soup!

Chicken Fajitas

SERVINGS: 4   **PREP TIME:** 20 MIN   **COOK TIME:** 25 MIN   **FREEZE-DRY TIME:** 24-48 HRS

Ingredients:

1 lb boneless, skinless chicken breasts, thinly sliced
2 tablespoons olive oil
1 onion, thinly sliced
1 bell pepper (any color), thinly sliced
2 cloves garlic, minced
1 tablespoon chili powder
1 teaspoon ground cumin
1/2 teaspoon smoked paprika
Salt and pepper to taste
Flour tortillas, for serving

Optional toppings: shredded cheese, salsa, sour cream, guacamole, chopped cilantro, lime wedges

Instructions:

1. Heat olive oil in a large skillet over medium-high heat.
2. Add thinly sliced chicken breasts to the skillet and season with chili powder, ground cumin, smoked paprika, salt, and pepper. Cook until chicken is cooked through and slightly browned, about 5-7 minutes. Remove chicken from skillet and set aside.
3. In the same skillet, add sliced onion and bell pepper. Cook until vegetables are tender and slightly charred, about 5-7 minutes.
4. Add minced garlic to the skillet and cook for an additional minute until fragrant.
5. Return the cooked chicken to the skillet and toss with the vegetables until heated through.
6. Serve the chicken and vegetable mixture hot with warm flour tortillas and your choice of toppings.

For Freeze-Drying:

- **Prepare**: Allow the Chicken Fajitas to cool completely after cooking. Portion the fajita mixture into individual servings.
- **Freeze**: Place the servings on freeze-drying trays, making sure they're not touching each other.
- **Freeze Dry**: Freeze dry the Chicken Fajitas at -40°F for 24 to 48 hours until completely dry.
- **Store**: Once dry, remove the freeze-dried servings from the trays and store them in airtight containers or vacuum-sealed bags.

Rehydrating:

- **Rehydrate**: To rehydrate the freeze-dried Chicken Fajitas, place a serving in a bowl or dish. Add enough hot water to cover the fajita mixture completely. Let the mixture soak in the hot water for about 10-15 minutes, stirring occasionally, until fully rehydrated and heated through.
- **Serve**: Drain any excess water, if necessary, and enjoy your rehydrated Chicken Fajitas!

Lemon Garlic Chicken Thighs

SERVINGS: 4   **PREP TIME:** 20 MIN   **COOK TIME:** 20 MIN   **FREEZE-DRY TIME:** 24-48 HRS

Ingredients:

4 bone-in, skin-on chicken thighs
2 tablespoons olive oil
4 cloves garlic, minced
Zest and juice of 1 lemon
1 teaspoon dried oregano
Salt and pepper to taste
Fresh parsley for garnish

Instructions:

1. Preheat your oven to 400°F.
2. Pat the chicken thighs dry with paper towels and season them generously with salt and pepper.
3. Heat olive oil in an oven-safe skillet over medium-high heat.
4. Place the chicken thighs skin side down in the skillet and cook until the skin is golden brown and crispy, about 5-7 minutes.
5. Flip the chicken thighs over and add minced garlic to the skillet. Cook for another minute until fragrant.
6. Remove the skillet from the heat and sprinkle lemon zest and dried oregano over the chicken thighs.
7. Squeeze lemon juice over the chicken thighs.
8. Transfer the skillet to the preheated oven and bake for 20-25 minutes, or until the chicken is cooked through and reaches an internal temperature of 165°F.
9. Remove from the oven and let the Lemon Garlic Chicken Thighs rest for a few minutes before serving.
10. Garnish with fresh parsley before serving.

For Freeze-Drying:

- **Prepare:** Allow the Lemon Garlic Chicken Thighs to cool completely after cooking. Portion the chicken thighs into individual servings.
- **Freeze:** Place the servings on freeze-drying trays, making sure they're not touching each other.
- **Freeze Dry:** Freeze dry the Lemon Garlic Chicken Thighs at -40°F for 24 to 48 hours until completely dry.
- **Store:** Once dry, remove the freeze-dried servings from the trays and store them in airtight containers or vacuum-sealed bags.

Rehydrating:

- **Rehydrate:** To rehydrate the freeze-dried Lemon Garlic Chicken Thighs, place a serving in a bowl or dish. Add enough hot water to cover the chicken completely. Let the chicken soak in the hot water for about 10-15 minutes, stirring occasionally, until fully rehydrated and heated through.
- **Serve:** Drain any excess water, if necessary, and enjoy your rehydrated Lemon Garlic Chicken Thighs!

Chapter Seven

Meals in a Jar

Chili and Cornbread Jar

SERVINGS: 4   **PREP TIME:** 15 MIN   **COOK TIME:** 30 MIN   **FREEZE-DRY TIME:** 24-48 HRS

Ingredients:

Ingredients for Chili:

1 lb ground beef
1 onion, chopped
2 cloves garlic, minced
1 bell pepper, diced
2 tablespoons chili powder
1 teaspoon ground cumin
Salt and pepper to taste
1 can (14 oz) diced tomatoes
1 can (14 oz) kidney beans, drained and rinsed
1 can (14 oz) black beans, drained and rinsed

Ingredients for Cornbread:

1 cup cornmeal
1 cup all-purpose flour
1/4 cup granulated sugar
1 tablespoon baking powder
1/2 teaspoon salt
1 cup milk
1/4 cup vegetable oil
1 egg

Optional toppings: shredded cheese, sour cream, sliced green onions

Instructions:

1. In a large skillet, cook the ground beef over medium heat until browned. Drain any excess fat.
2. Add chopped onion, minced garlic, and diced bell pepper to the skillet. Cook until vegetables are softened, about 5-7 minutes.
3. Stir in diced tomatoes, kidney beans, black beans, chili powder, ground cumin, salt, and pepper. Simmer the chi for 15-20 minutes to allow the flavors to meld together. Remove from heat.
4. In a separate bowl, whisk together cornmeal, flour, sugar, baking powder, and salt.
5. In another bowl, whisk together milk, vegetable oil, and egg.
6. Pour the wet ingredients into the dry ingredients and stir until just combined. Do not overmix.

To assemble the Chili and Cornbread Jar:

1. Spoon the chili mixture into jars, filling them halfway.
2. Top the chili with spoonfuls of cornbread batter, filling the jars up to 3/4 full.
3. Secure the lids on the jars and freeze the Chili and Cornbread Jars until ready to use.

For Freeze-Drying:

- **Prepare:** Allow the Chili and Cornbread Jars to freeze completely.
- **Freeze:** Once frozen, remove the jars from the freezer and place them in a freeze dryer.
- **Freeze Dry:** Freeze dry the Chili and Cornbread Jars at -40°F for 24 to 48 hours until completely dry.
- **Store:** Once dry, remove the jars from the freeze dryer and store them in a cool, dry place.

Rehydrating:

- **Rehydrate:** To rehydrate the freeze-dried Chili and Cornbread Jars, remove the lids from the jars. Add hot water to the jars, filling them to just below the rim. Stir the contents of the jars to combine the chili and cornbread. Let the jars sit for about 10-15 minutes, stirring occasionally, until fully rehydrated and heated through.
- **Serve:** Enjoy your rehydrated Chili and Cornbread straight from the jars, or pour them into bowls and top with optional toppings like shredded cheese, sour cream, and sliced green onions.

Chicken Alfredo Pasta Jar

SERVINGS: 4   **PREP TIME:** 15 MIN   **COOK TIME:** 15 MIN   **FREEZE-DRY TIME:** 24-48 HRS

Ingredients:

8 oz fettuccine pasta
1 lb boneless, skinless chicken breasts, cut into bite-sized pieces
2 tablespoons olive oil
2 cloves garlic, minced
1 cup heavy cream
1/2 cup grated Parmesan cheese
Salt and pepper to taste
Fresh parsley for garnish

Instructions:

1. Cook the fettuccine pasta according to package instructions until al dente. Drain and set aside.
2. Heat olive oil in a large skillet over medium-high heat. Add minced garlic and cook until fragrant, about 1 minute.
3. Add the bite-sized chicken pieces to the skillet and cook until browned and cooked through, about 5-7 minutes.
4. Reduce the heat to medium-low. Pour in heavy cream and grated Parmesan cheese, stirring until the cheese is melted and the sauce is smooth.
5. Season the Alfredo sauce with salt and pepper to taste.
6. Add the cooked fettuccine pasta to the skillet, tossing until the pasta is evenly coated with the Alfredo sauce.
7. Let the Chicken Alfredo Pasta cool slightly.

To assemble the Chicken Alfredo Pasta Jar:

1. Spoon the cooled Chicken Alfredo Pasta into a jar, filling it about halfway.
2. Seal the jar tightly with a lid.

For Freeze-Drying:

- **Prepare**: Allow the Chicken Alfredo Pasta Jars to freeze completely.
- **Freeze**: Once frozen, remove the jars from the freezer and place them in a freeze dryer.
- **Freeze Dry**: Freeze dry the Chicken Alfredo Pasta Jars at -40°F for 24 to 48 hours until completely dry.
- **Store**: Once dry, remove the jars from the freeze dryer and store them in a cool, dry place.

Rehydrating:

- **Rehydrate**: To rehydrate the freeze-dried Chicken Alfredo Pasta Jars, remove the lids from the jars. Add hot water to the jars, filling them to just below the rim. Stir the contents of the jars to combine the pasta and sauce. Let the jars sit for about 10-15 minutes, stirring occasionally, until fully rehydrated and heated through.
- **Serve**: Enjoy your rehydrated Chicken Alfredo Pasta straight from the jars, or pour them into bowls and garnish with fresh parsley before serving.

Beef Stroganoff Jar

SERVINGS: 4   **PREP TIME:** 15 MIN   **COOK TIME:** 20 MIN   **FREEZE-DRY TIME:** 24-48 HRS

Ingredients:

- 1 lb beef sirloin steak, thinly sliced
- Salt and pepper to taste
- 2 tablespoons olive oil
- 1 onion, chopped
- 2 cloves garlic, minced
- 8 oz mushrooms, sliced
- 2 tablespoons all-purpose flour
- 1 cup beef broth
- 1 cup sour cream
- 1 tablespoon Worcestershire sauce
- 8 oz egg noodles, cooked according to package instructions
- **Fresh parsley for garnish**

Instructions:

1. Season the thinly sliced beef sirloin steak with salt and pepper.
2. Heat olive oil in a large skillet over medium-high heat. Add the seasoned beef slices and cook until browned on both sides, about 3-4 minutes per side. Remove the beef from the skillet and set aside.
3. In the same skillet, add chopped onion and minced garlic. Cook until onion is softened, about 5 minutes.
4. Add sliced mushrooms to the skillet and cook until they release their moisture and are browned about 5-7 minutes.
5. Sprinkle all-purpose flour over the vegetables in the skillet and stir to coat.
6. Slowly pour in beef broth, stirring constantly to prevent lumps from forming. Cook until the sauce thickens, about 2-3 minutes.
7. Return the cooked beef slices to the skillet. Stir in sour cream and Worcestershire sauce until well combined. Cook for an additional 2-3 minutes, until the beef is heated through and the sauce is creamy.
8. Remove the skillet from heat and let the Beef Stroganoff cool slightly.

To assemble the Beef Stroganoff Jar:

1. Spoon the cooled Beef Stroganoff into a jar, filling it about halfway.
2. Add a layer of cooked egg noodles on top of the Beef Stroganoff.
3. Seal the jar tightly with a lid.

For Freeze-Drying:

- **Prepare**: Allow the Beef Stroganoff Jars to freeze completely.
- **Freeze**: Once frozen, remove the jars from the freezer and place them in a freeze dryer.
- **Freeze Dry**: Freeze dry the Beef Stroganoff Jars at -40°F for 24 to 48 hours until completely dry.
- **Store**: Once dry, remove the jars from the freeze dryer and store them in a cool, dry place.

Rehydrating:

- **Rehydrate**: To rehydrate the freeze-dried Beef Stroganoff Jars, remove the lids from the jars. Add hot water to the jars, filling them to just below the rim. Stir the contents of the jars to combine the beef stroganoff and noodles. Let the jars sit for about 10-15 minutes, stirring occasionally, until fully rehydrated and heated through.
- **Serve**: Enjoy your rehydrated Beef Stroganoff straight from the jars, or pour them into bowls and garnish with fresh parsley before serving.

Vegetable Soup Jar

SERVINGS: 4   **PREP TIME:** 15 MIN   **COOK TIME:** 30 MIN   **FREEZE-DRY TIME:** 24-48 HRS

Ingredients:

- 2 tablespoons olive oil
- 1 onion, chopped
- 2 carrots, diced
- 2 celery stalks, diced
- 2 cloves garlic, minced
- 1 can (14 oz) diced tomatoes
- 4 cups vegetable broth
- 1 cup frozen corn kernels
- 1 cup frozen green beans
- 1 cup frozen peas
- 1 teaspoon dried thyme
- Salt and pepper to taste
- **Fresh parsley for garnish (optional)**

Instructions:

1. Heat olive oil in a large pot over medium heat. Add chopped onion, diced carrots, and diced celery. Cook until vegetables are softened, about 5-7 minutes.
2. Add minced garlic to the pot and cook for an additional minute until fragrant.
3. Pour in diced tomatoes (with their juices) and vegetable broth. Bring the soup to a simmer.
4. Stir in frozen corn kernels, green beans, and peas. Add dried thyme, salt, and pepper to taste.
5. Simmer the Vegetable Soup for 15-20 minutes to allow the flavors to meld together.
6. Taste and adjust seasoning if necessary.
7. Let the Vegetable Soup cool slightly.

To assemble the Vegetable Soup Jar:

1. Spoon the cooled Vegetable Soup into a jar, filling it about halfway.
2. Seal the jar tightly with a lid.

For Freeze-Drying:

- **Prepare**: Allow the Vegetable Soup Jars to freeze completely.
- **Freeze**: Once frozen, remove the jars from the freezer and place them in a freeze dryer.
- **Freeze Dry**: Freeze dry the Vegetable Soup Jars at -40°F for 24 to 48 hours until completely dry.
- **Store**: Once dry, remove the jars from the freeze dryer and store them in a cool, dry place.

Rehydrating:

- **Rehydrate**: To rehydrate the freeze-dried Vegetable Soup Jars, remove the lids from the jars. Add hot water to the jars, filling them to just below the rim. Stir the contents of the jars to combine the soup. Let the jars sit for about 10-15 minutes, stirring occasionally, until fully rehydrated and heated through.
- **Serve**: Enjoy your rehydrated Vegetable Soup straight from the jars, or pour them into bowls and garnish with fresh parsley before serving.

Mexican Rice and Bean Jar

SERVINGS: 4   **PREP TIME:** 15 MIN   **COOK TIME:** 30 MIN   **FREEZE-DRY TIME:** 24-48 HRS

Ingredients:

1 cup long-grain white rice
1 tablespoon olive oil
1 onion, chopped
2 cloves garlic, minced
1 can (14 oz) diced tomatoes
1 can (15 oz) black beans, drained and rinsed
1 cup frozen corn kernels
1 teaspoon ground cumin
1 teaspoon chili powder
Salt and pepper to taste
2 cups vegetable broth
Fresh cilantro for garnish (optional)

Instructions:

1. Rinse the white rice under cold water until the water runs clear. Drain and set aside.
2. Heat olive oil in a large pot over medium heat. Add chopped onion and minced garlic. Cook until onion is softened, about 5 minutes.
3. Add the rinsed white rice to the pot and stir to coat with the onion and garlic mixture.
4. Pour in diced tomatoes (with their juices), black beans, frozen corn kernels, ground cumin, chili powder, salt, and pepper. Stir to combine.
5. Add vegetable broth to the pot and bring the mixture to a boil.
6. Reduce the heat to low, cover the pot, and simmer for 15-20 minutes, or until the rice is cooked and the liquid is absorbed.
7. Remove the pot from heat and let the Mexican Rice and Bean mixture cool slightly.

To assemble the Mexican Rice and Bean Jar:

1. Spoon the cooled Mexican Rice and Bean mixture into a jar, filling it about halfway.
2. Seal the jar tightly with a lid.

For Freeze-Drying:

- **Prepare**: Allow the Mexican Rice and Bean Jars to freeze completely.
- **Freeze**: Once frozen, remove the jars from the freezer and place them in a freeze dryer.
- **Freeze Dry**: Freeze dry the Mexican Rice and Bean Jars at -40°F for 24 to 48 hours until completely dry.
- **Store**: Once dry, remove the jars from the freeze dryer and store them in a cool, dry place.

Rehydrating:

- **Rehydrate**: To rehydrate the freeze-dried Mexican Rice and Bean Jars, remove the lids from the jars. Add hot water to the jars, filling them to just below the rim. Stir the contents of the jars to combine the rice and bean mixture. Let the jars sit for about 10-15 minutes, stirring occasionally, until fully rehydrated and heated through.
- **Serve**: Enjoy your rehydrated Mexican Rice and Bean straight from the jars, or pour them into bowls and garnish with fresh cilantro before serving.

Curry Rice Jar

SERVINGS: 4   **PREP TIME:** 15 MIN   **COOK TIME:** 30 MIN   **FREEZE-DRY TIME:** 24-48 HRS

Ingredients:

1 cup basmati rice
1 tablespoon vegetable oil
1 onion, chopped
2 cloves garlic, minced
1 bell pepper, diced
1 carrot, diced
1 tablespoon curry powder
1 teaspoon ground turmeric
1 can (14 oz) coconut milk
1 cup vegetable broth

Salt and pepper to taste
Fresh cilantro for garnish (optional)

Instructions:

1. Rinse the basmati rice under cold water until the water runs clear. Drain and set aside.
2. Heat vegetable oil in a large pot over medium heat. Add chopped onion and minced garlic. Cook until onion is softened, about 5 minutes.
3. Add diced bell pepper and diced carrot to the pot. Cook for another 5 minutes, until vegetables are slightly softened.
4. Stir in curry powder and ground turmeric, and cook for 1-2 minutes until fragrant.
5. Add rinsed basmati rice to the pot and stir to coat with the spice mixture.
6. Pour in coconut milk and vegetable broth. Season with salt and pepper to taste. Stir to combine.
7. Bring the mixture to a boil, then reduce the heat to low, cover the pot, and simmer for 15-20 minutes, or until the rice is cooked and the liquid is absorbed.
8. Remove the pot from heat and let the Curry Rice mixture cool slightly.

To assemble the Curry Rice Jar:

1. Spoon the cooled Curry Rice mixture into a jar, filling it about halfway.
2. Seal the jar tightly with a lid.

For Freeze-Drying:

- **Prepare**: Allow the Curry Rice Jars to freeze completely.
- **Freeze**: Once frozen, remove the jars from the freezer and place them in a freeze dryer.
- **Freeze Dry**: Freeze dry the Curry Rice Jars at -40°F for 24 to 48 hours until completely dry.
- **Store**: Once dry, remove the jars from the freeze dryer and store them in a cool, dry place.

Rehydrating:

- **Rehydrate**: To rehydrate the freeze-dried Curry Rice Jars, remove the lids from the jars. Add hot water to the jars, filling them to just below the rim. Stir the contents of the jars to combine the rice and curry mixture. Let the jars sit for about 10-15 minutes, stirring occasionally, until fully rehydrated and heated through.
- **Serve**: Enjoy your rehydrated Curry Rice straight from the jars, or pour them into bowls and garnish with fresh cilantro before serving.

Oatmeal Breakfast Jar

SERVINGS: 4   **PREP TIME:** 10 MIN   **COOK TIME:** 0 MIN   **FREEZE-DRY TIME:** 24-48 HRS

Ingredients:

1 cup old-fashioned oats
2 cups milk (dairy or non-dairy)
2 tablespoons maple syrup or honey
1 teaspoon ground cinnamon
1/4 teaspoon salt
1/2 cup chopped nuts or seeds (such as almonds, walnuts, or pumpkin seeds)
1/2 cup dried fruit (such as raisins, cranberries, or chopped apricots)

Optional toppings: fresh fruit, yogurt, nut butter, coconut flakes

Instructions:

1. In a large bowl, combine old-fashioned oats, milk, maple syrup or honey, ground cinnamon, and salt.
2. Stir until well combined.
3. Add chopped nuts or seeds and dried fruit to the oat mixture. Stir to distribute evenly.

To assemble the Oatmeal Breakfast Jar:

1. Divide the oat mixture into individual jars or containers, leaving some space at the top for toppings.
2. Seal the jars or containers tightly with lids.

For Freeze-Drying:

- **Prepare**: Allow the Oatmeal Breakfast Jars to freeze completely.
- **Freeze**: Once frozen, remove the jars from the freezer and place them in a freeze dryer.
- **Freeze Dry**: Freeze dry the Oatmeal Breakfast Jars at -40°F for 24 to 48 hours until completely dry.
- **Store**: Once dry, remove the jars from the freeze dryer and store them in a cool, dry place.

Rehydrating:

- **Rehydrate**: To rehydrate, remove the lids from the jars. Add hot water to the jars, filling them to just below the rim. Stir the contents of the jars to combine the oat mixture. Let the jars sit for about 5-10 minutes, stirring occasionally, until fully rehydrated and heated through.
- **Serve**: Top the rehydrated oatmeal with your favorite toppings, such as fresh fruit, yogurt, nut butter, or coconut flakes, and enjoy!

Quinoa Salad Jar

SERVINGS: 4   **PREP TIME:** 10 MIN   **COOK TIME:** 20 MIN   **FREEZE-DRY TIME:** 24-48 HRS

Ingredients:

1 cup quinoa, rinsed
2 cups water or vegetable broth
1 cup cherry tomatoes, halved
1 cucumber, diced
1 bell pepper, diced
1/4 cup red onion, finely chopped
1/4 cup fresh parsley, chopped
1/4 cup feta cheese, crumbled (optional)
2 tablespoons olive oil
2 tablespoons lemon juice
Salt and pepper to taste

Optional toppings: fresh fruit, yogurt, nut butter, coconut flakes

Instructions:

1. In a medium saucepan, combine quinoa and water or vegetable broth. Bring to a boil, then reduce heat to low and simmer, covered, for 15-20 minutes, or until quinoa is cooked and water is absorbed. Remove from heat and let cool.
2. In a large bowl, combine cooked quinoa, cherry tomatoes, cucumber, bell pepper, red onion, and fresh parsley. Toss to combine.
3. In a small bowl, whisk together olive oil, lemon juice, salt, and pepper to make the dressing.
4. Pour the dressing over the quinoa salad and toss to coat evenly. Add crumbled feta cheese if desired.

To assemble the Quinoa Salad Jar:

1. Divide the quinoa salad into individual jars or containers, leaving some space at the top for toppings.
2. Seal the jars or containers tightly with lids.

For Freeze-Drying:

- **Prepare**: Allow the Quinoa Salad Jars to freeze completely.
- **Freeze**: Once frozen, remove the jars from the freezer and place them in a freeze dryer.
- **Freeze Dry**: Freeze dry the Quinoa Salad Jars at -40°F for 24 to 48 hours until completely dry.
- **Store**: Once dry, remove the jars from the freeze dryer and store them in a cool, dry place.

Rehydrating:

- **Rehydrate**: To rehydrate the freeze-dried Quinoa Salad Jars, remove the lids from the jars. Add hot water to the jars, filling them to just below the rim. Stir the contents of the jars to combine the quinoa salad. Let the jars sit for about 5-10 minutes, stirring occasionally, until fully rehydrated and heated through.
- **Serve**: Enjoy your rehydrated Quinoa Salad straight from the jars, or pour them into bowls and serve as a side dish or light meal.

Mushroom Risotto Jar

SERVINGS: 4   **PREP TIME:** 15 MIN   **COOK TIME:** 35 MIN   **FREEZE-DRY TIME:** 24-48 HRS

Ingredients:

1 cup Arborio rice
2 cups vegetable broth
1 tablespoon olive oil
1 onion, finely chopped
2 cloves garlic, minced
8 oz mushrooms, sliced
1/4 cup white wine (optional)
1/4 cup grated Parmesan cheese
Salt and pepper to taste
Fresh parsley for garnish (optional)

Instructions:

1. In a medium saucepan, heat vegetable broth over medium heat until simmering. Reduce heat to low to keep warm.
2. In a large skillet, heat olive oil over medium heat. Add chopped onion and minced garlic. Cook until onion is softened, about 5 minutes.
3. Add sliced mushrooms to the skillet and cook until they release their moisture and are browned about 5-7 minutes.
4. Stir in Arborio rice and cook for 1-2 minutes, until the rice is lightly toasted.
5. If using white wine, pour it into the skillet and stir until absorbed by the rice.
6. Begin adding the warm vegetable broth to the skillet, one ladleful at a time, stirring frequently and allowing the rice to absorb the broth before adding more. Continue this process until the rice is creamy and tender, about 20-25 minutes.
7. Stir in grated Parmesan cheese until melted and well combined. Season with salt and pepper to taste.
8. Remove the skillet from heat and let the Mushroom Risotto cool slightly.

To assemble the Mushroom Risotto Jar:

1. Spoon the cooled Mushroom Risotto into a jar, filling it about halfway.
2. Seal the jar tightly with a lid.

For Freeze-Drying:

- **Prepare**: Allow the Mushroom Risotto Jars to freeze completely.
- **Freeze**: Once frozen, remove the jars from the freezer and place them in a freeze dryer.
- **Freeze Dry**: Freeze dry the Mushroom Risotto Jars at -40°F for 24 to 48 hours until completely dry.
- **Store**: Once dry, remove the jars from the freeze dryer and store them in a cool, dry place.

Rehydrating:

- **Rehydrate**: To rehydrate the freeze-dried Mushroom Risotto Jars, remove the lids from the jars. Add hot water to the jars, filling them to just below the rim. Stir the contents of the jars to combine the risotto. Let the jars sit for about 10-15 minutes, stirring occasionally, until fully rehydrated and heated through.
- **Serve**: Garnish with fresh parsley before serving, if desired.

Chicken Noodle Soup Jar

SERVINGS: 4   **PREP TIME:** 15 MIN   **COOK TIME:** 20 MIN   **FREEZE-DRY TIME:** 24-48 HRS

Ingredients:

1 cup uncooked egg noodles
1 cup cooked chicken, shredded or diced
2 carrots, sliced
2 celery stalks, sliced
1/2 onion, diced
2 cloves garlic, minced
4 cups chicken broth
1 teaspoon dried thyme
Salt and pepper to taste
Fresh parsley for garnish (optional)

Instructions:

1. In a large pot, bring chicken broth to a simmer over medium heat.
2. Add sliced carrots, sliced celery, diced onion, minced garlic, and dried thyme to the pot. Simmer for 10-15 minutes or until vegetables are tender.
3. Add uncooked egg noodles to the pot and cook according to package instructions, usually about 6-8 minutes.
4. Stir in cooked chicken and simmer for an additional 2-3 minutes or until chicken is heated through.
5. Season with salt and pepper to taste.
6. Remove the pot from heat and let the Chicken Noodle Soup cool slightly.

To assemble the Chicken Noodle Soup Jar:

1. Spoon the cooled Chicken Noodle Soup into a jar, filling it about halfway.
2. Seal the jar tightly with a lid.

For Freeze-Drying:

- **Prepare**: Allow the Chicken Noodle Soup Jars to freeze completely.
- **Freeze**: Once frozen, remove the jars from the freezer and place them in a freeze dryer.
- **Freeze Dry**: Freeze dry the Chicken Noodle Soup Jars at -40°F for 24 to 48 hours until completely dry.
- **Store**: Once dry, remove the jars from the freeze dryer and store them in a cool, dry place.

Rehydrating:

- **Rehydrate**: To rehydrate, remove the lids from the jars. Add hot water to the jars, filling them to just below the rim. Stir the contents of the jars to combine the soup. Let the jars sit for about 10-15 minutes, stirring occasionally, until fully rehydrated and heated through.
- **Serve**: Garnish with fresh parsley before serving, if desired.

Minestrone Soup Jar

SERVINGS: 4 **PREP TIME:** 15 MIN **COOK TIME:** 30 MIN **FREEZE-DRY TIME:** 24-48 HRS

Ingredients:

- 1 cup small pasta (such as ditalini or shells)
- 2 tablespoons olive oil
- 1 onion, diced
- 2 carrots, diced
- 2 celery stalks, diced
- 2 cloves garlic, minced
- 1 can (14 oz) diced tomatoes
- 4 cups vegetable broth
- 1 can (15 oz) cannellini beans, drained and rinsed
- 1 zucchini, diced
- 1 cup chopped spinach or kale
- 1 teaspoon dried thyme
- 1 teaspoon dried oregano
- Salt and pepper to taste
- **Grated Parmesan cheese for garnish (optional)**

Instructions:

1. Cook the small pasta according to package instructions until al dente. Drain and set aside.
2. In a large pot, heat olive oil over medium heat. Add diced onion, carrots, and celery. Cook until vegetables are softened, about 5-7 minutes.
3. Add minced garlic to the pot and cook for an additional minute until fragrant.
4. Pour in diced tomatoes (with their juices) and vegetable broth. Bring the soup to a simmer.
5. Stir in drained and rinsed cannellini beans, diced zucchini, chopped spinach or kale, dried thyme, and dried oregano. Season with salt and pepper to taste.
6. Simmer the Minestrone Soup for 15-20 minutes to allow the flavors to meld together.
7. Remove the pot from heat and let the soup cool slightly.

To assemble the Minestrone Soup Jar:

1. Spoon the cooled Minestrone Soup into a jar, filling it about halfway.
2. Add a layer of cooked small pasta on top of the soup.
3. Seal the jar tightly with a lid.

For Freeze-Drying:

- **Prepare:** Allow the Minestrone Soup Jars to freeze completely.
- **Freeze:** Once frozen, remove the jars from the freezer and place them in a freeze dryer.
- **Freeze Dry:** Freeze dry the Minestrone Soup Jars at -40°F for 24 to 48 hours until completely dry.
- **Store:** Once dry, remove the jars from the freeze dryer and store them in a cool, dry place.

Rehydrating:

- **Rehydrate:** To rehydrate, remove the lids from the jars. Add hot water to the jars, filling them to just below the rim. Stir the contents of the jars to combine the soup and pasta. Let the jars sit for about 10-15 minutes, stirring occasionally, until fully rehydrated and heated through.
- **Serve:** Serve the soup topped with grated Parmesan cheese, if desired.

Thai Peanut Noodle Jar

SERVINGS: 4   **PREP TIME:** 15 MIN   **COOK TIME:** 15 MIN   **FREEZE-DRY TIME:** 24-48 HRS

Ingredients:

- 8 oz rice noodles
- 1/4 cup peanut butter
- 2 tablespoons soy sauce
- 1 tablespoon sesame oil
- 1 tablespoon rice vinegar
- 1 tablespoon honey or maple syrup
- 1 clove garlic, minced
- 1 teaspoon grated ginger
- 1/4 teaspoon red pepper flakes (optional)
- 1 carrot, julienned
- 1/2 red bell pepper, thinly sliced
- 1/2 cucumber, thinly sliced
- 2 green onions, thinly sliced
- 1/4 cup chopped cilantro (optional)
- **Crushed peanuts for garnish (optional)**
- **Lime wedges for serving (optional)**

Instructions:

1. Cook the rice noodles according to package instructions until al dente. Drain and rinse with cold water to stop the cooking process. Set aside.
2. In a small bowl, whisk together peanut butter, soy sauce, sesame oil, rice vinegar, honey or maple syrup, minced garlic, grated ginger, and red pepper flakes (if using) until smooth. Set aside.
3. Divide the cooked rice noodles evenly among jars.
4. Layer the julienned carrot, sliced red bell pepper, sliced cucumber, green onions, and chopped cilantro (if using) on top of the rice noodles in each jar.

To assemble the Thai Peanut Noodle Jar:

1. Pour the prepared peanut sauce evenly over the ingredients in each jar.
2. Seal the jars tightly with lids.

For Freeze-Drying:

- **Prepare**: Allow the Thai Peanut Noodle Jars to freeze completely.
- **Freeze**: Once frozen, remove the jars from the freezer and place them in a freeze dryer.
- **Freeze Dry**: Freeze dry the Thai Peanut Noodle Jars at -40°F for 24 to 48 hours until completely dry.
- **Store**: Once dry, remove the jars from the freeze dryer and store them in a cool, dry place.

Rehydrating:

- **Rehydrate**: To rehydrate, remove the lids from the jars. Add hot water to the jars, filling them to just below the rim. Stir the contents of the jars to combine the noodles, vegetables, and peanut sauce. Let the jars sit for about 10-15 minutes, stirring occasionally, until fully rehydrated and heated through.
- **Serve**: Garnish with crushed peanuts and serve with lime wedges, if desired.

Taco Soup Jar

SERVINGS: 4   **PREP TIME:** 20 MIN   **COOK TIME:** 0 MIN   **FREEZE-DRY TIME:** 24-48 HRS

Ingredients:

1/2 cup cooked, dried black beans
1/2 cup cooked, dried kidney beans
1/2 cup cooked, dried pinto beans
1 cup frozen corn kernels
1 can (14 oz) diced tomatoes
1 packet taco seasoning mix
1/4 cup diced green chilies (optional)
1/4 cup diced onion
1/4 cup diced bell pepper (any color)
2 cloves garlic, minced
Salt and pepper to taste
Crushed tortilla chips for serving (optional)

Shredded cheese for serving (optional)
Sour cream for serving (optional)
Fresh cilantro for garnish (optional)
Lime wedges for serving (optional)

Instructions:

1. Rinse the dried beans under cold water and drain.
2. Add the beans to the jar and tamp them down.
3. Layer the dried beans, frozen corn kernels, diced tomatoes, taco seasoning mix, diced green chilies (if using), diced onion, diced bell pepper, and minced garlic in jars, dividing evenly.
4. Seal the jars tightly with lids.

For Freeze-Drying:

- **Prepare**: Allow the Taco Soup Jars to freeze completely.
- **Freeze**: Once frozen, remove the jars from the freezer and place them in a freeze dryer.
- **Freeze Dry**: Freeze dry the Taco Soup Jars at -40°F for 24 to 48 hours until completely dry.
- **Store**: Once dry, remove the jars from the freeze dryer and store them in a cool, dry place.

Rehydrating:

- **Rehydrate**: To rehydrate, remove the lids from the jars. Add hot water to the jars, filling them to just below the rim. Stir the contents of the jars to combine the ingredients. Let the jars sit for about 10-15 minutes, stirring occasionally, until fully rehydrated and heated through.
- **Serve**: Serve the soup topped with crushed tortilla chips, shredded cheese, sour cream, fresh cilantro, and lime wedges, if desired.

BBQ Chicken Rice Jar

SERVINGS: 4   **PREP TIME:** 15 MIN   **COOK TIME:** 15 MIN   **FREEZE-DRY TIME:** 24-48 HRS

Ingredients:

1 cup cooked chicken, shredded or diced
1 cup cooked rice (white or brown)
1/2 cup barbecue sauce
1/4 cup diced red bell pepper
1/4 cup diced green bell pepper
1/4 cup diced onion
1/4 cup canned corn kernels, drained
1/4 cup canned black beans, drained and rinsed
Salt and pepper to taste

Shredded cheese for topping (optional)
Chopped green onions for garnish (optional)

Instructions:

1. In a bowl, combine the cooked chicken, cooked rice, barbecue sauce, diced red bell pepper, diced green bell pepper, diced onion, canned corn kernels, and canned black beans.
2. Mix well to combine.
3. Divide the BBQ chicken rice mixture evenly among jars.
4. Seal the jars tightly with lids.

For Freeze-Drying:

- **Prepare**: Allow the BBQ Chicken Rice Jars to freeze completely.
- **Freeze**: Once frozen, remove the jars from the freezer and place them in a freeze dryer.
- **Freeze Dry**: Freeze dry the BBQ Chicken Rice Jars at -40°F for 24 to 48 hours until completely dry.
- **Store**: Once dry, remove the jars from the freeze dryer and store them in a cool, dry place.

Rehydrating:

- **Rehydrate**: To rehydrate, remove the lids from the jars. Add hot water to the jars, filling them to just below the rim. Stir the contents of the jars to combine the ingredients. Let the jars sit for about 10-15 minutes, stirring occasionally, until fully rehydrated and heated through.
- **Serve**: Top the rehydrated BBQ chicken rice with shredded cheese and chopped green onions, if desired.

Lentil Stew Jar

SERVINGS: 4   **PREP TIME:** 15 MIN   **COOK TIME:** 15 MIN   **FREEZE-DRY TIME:** 24-48 HRS

Ingredients:

1 cup cooked, dried lentils
1 onion, diced
2 carrots, diced
2 celery stalks, diced
2 cloves garlic, minced
1 can (14 oz) diced tomatoes
4 cups vegetable broth
1 teaspoon dried thyme
1 teaspoon dried oregano
Salt and pepper to taste
Fresh parsley for garnish (optional)

Instructions:

1. Rinse the dried lentils under cold water and drain.
2. Layer the dried lentils, diced onion, diced carrots, diced celery, minced garlic, diced tomatoes (with their juices), dried thyme, and dried oregano in jars, dividing evenly.
3. Pour vegetable broth over the ingredients in each jar.
4. Seal the jars tightly with lids.

For Freeze-Drying:

- **Prepare**: Allow the Lentil Stew Jars to freeze completely.
- **Freeze**: Once frozen, remove the jars from the freezer and place them in a freeze dryer.
- **Freeze Dry**: Freeze dry the Lentil Stew Jars at -40°F for 24 to 48 hours until completely dry.
- **Store**: Once dry, remove the jars from the freeze dryer and store them in a cool, dry place.

Rehydrating:

- **Rehydrate**: To rehydrate, remove the lids from the jars. Add hot water to the jars, filling them to just below the rim. Stir the contents of the jars to combine the ingredients. Let the jars sit for about 10-15 minutes, stirring occasionally, until fully rehydrated and heated through.
- **Serve**: Garnish with fresh parsley before serving, if desired.

Spanish Rice Jar

SERVINGS: 4   **PREP TIME:** 15 MIN   **COOK TIME:** 5 MIN   **FREEZE-DRY TIME:** 24-48 HRS

Ingredients:

1 cup long-grain white rice, cooked
1 can (14 oz) diced tomatoes
1 onion, diced
1 bell pepper, diced
2 cloves garlic, minced
1 teaspoon ground cumin
1 teaspoon paprika
1/2 teaspoon chili powder
Salt and pepper to taste
Fresh cilantro for garnish (optional)

Instructions:

1. Rinse the rice under cold water and drain.
2. Layer the rinsed rice, diced tomatoes (with their juices), diced onion, diced bell pepper, minced garlic, ground cumin, paprika, chili powder, salt, and pepper in jars, dividing evenly.
3. Seal the jars tightly with lids.

For Freeze-Drying:

- **Prepare**: Allow the Spanish Rice Jars to freeze completely.
- **Freeze**: Once frozen, remove the jars from the freezer and place them in a freeze dryer.
- **Freeze Dry**: Freeze dry the Spanish Rice Jars at -40°F for 24 to 48 hours until completely dry.
- **Store**: Once dry, remove the jars from the freeze dryer and store them in a cool, dry place.

Rehydrating:

- **Rehydrate**: To rehydrate, remove the lids from the jars. Add hot water to the jars, filling them to just below the rim. Stir the contents of the jars to combine the ingredients. Let the jars sit for about 10-15 minutes, stirring occasionally, until fully rehydrated and heated through.
- **Serve**: Garnish with fresh cilantro before serving, if desired.

Macaroni and Cheese Jar

SERVINGS: 4   **PREP TIME:** 15 MIN   **COOK TIME:** 20 MIN   **FREEZE-DRY TIME:** 24-48 HRS

Ingredients:

1 cup uncooked macaroni pasta
2 tablespoons butter
2 tablespoons all-purpose flour
1 1/2 cups milk
2 cups shredded cheddar cheese
Salt and pepper to taste

Optional add-ins: cooked bacon, diced ham, cooked broccoli florets, diced bell peppers

Instructions:

1. Cook the macaroni pasta according to package instructions until al dente. Drain and set aside.
2. Melt the butter in a saucepan over medium heat. Add the flour and whisk continuously for 1-2 minutes to make a roux.
3. Gradually pour in the milk while whisking constantly to avoid lumps. Cook until the mixture thickens and begins to simmer.
4. Reduce heat to low and stir in the shredded cheddar cheese until melted and smooth. Season with salt and pepper to taste.
5. Add the cooked macaroni pasta to the cheese sauce and stir to coat evenly. If using optional add-ins, stir them in at this point.
6. Let the macaroni and cheese mixture cool slightly.

To assemble the Macaroni and Cheese Jar:

1. Spoon the cooled macaroni and cheese mixture into a jar, filling it about halfway.
2. Seal the jar tightly with a lid.

For Freeze-Drying:

- **Prepare:** Allow the Macaroni and Cheese Jars to freeze completely.
- **Freeze:** Once frozen, remove the jars from the freezer and place them in a freeze dryer.
- **Freeze Dry:** Freeze dry the Macaroni and Cheese Jars at -40°F for 24 to 48 hours until completely dry.
- **Store:** Once dry, remove the jars from the freeze dryer and store them in a cool, dry place.

Rehydrating:

- **Rehydrate:** To rehydrate, remove the lids from the jars. Add hot water to the jars, filling them to just below the rim. Stir the contents of the jars to combine the macaroni and cheese. Let the jars sit for about 10-15 minutes, stirring occasionally, until fully rehydrated and heated through.
- **Serve:** Serve the rehydrated macaroni and cheese warm.

Shepherd's Pie Jar

SERVINGS: 4   **PREP TIME:** 15 MIN   **COOK TIME:** 20 MIN   **FREEZE-DRY TIME:** 24-48 HRS

Ingredients:

1 lb ground beef or lamb
1 onion, diced
2 carrots, diced
2 celery stalks, diced
2 cloves garlic, minced
1 cup frozen peas
1 cup beef or vegetable broth
2 tablespoons tomato paste
2 tablespoons Worcestershire sauce
Salt and pepper to taste
2 cups mashed potatoes (prepared or instant)

Instructions:

1. In a large skillet, brown the ground beef or lamb over medium heat until cooked through. Drain excess fat if needed.
2. Add diced onion, diced carrots, diced celery, and minced garlic to the skillet with the cooked meat. Cook until vegetables are softened, about 5-7 minutes.
3. Stir in frozen peas, beef or vegetable broth, tomato paste, and Worcestershire sauce. Season with salt and pepper to taste. Simmer for 10-15 minutes until the mixture has thickened slightly.
4. Remove the skillet from heat and let the filling cool slightly.

To assemble the Shepherd's Pie Jar:

1. Spoon the cooled filling into jars, filling them about halfway.
2. Top each jar with a layer of mashed potatoes, dividing evenly.
3. Seal the jars tightly with lids.

For Freeze-Drying:

- **Prepare:** Allow the Shepherd's Pie Jars to freeze completely.
- **Freeze:** Once frozen, remove the jars from the freezer and place them in a freeze dryer.
- **Freeze Dry:** Freeze dry the Shepherd's Pie Jars at -40°F for 24 to 48 hours until completely dry.
- **Store:** Once dry, remove the jars from the freeze dryer and store them in a cool, dry place.

Rehydrating:

- **Rehydrate:** To rehydrate, remove the lids from the jars. Add hot water to the jars, filling them to just below the rim. Stir the contents of the jars to combine the filling and mashed potatoes. Let the jars sit for about 10-15 minutes, stirring occasionally, until fully rehydrated and heated through.
- **Serve:** Serve the rehydrated Shepherd's Pie warm.

Breakfast Scramble Jar

SERVINGS: 4   **PREP TIME:** 15 MIN   **COOK TIME:** 20 MIN   **FREEZE-DRY TIME:** 24-48 HRS

Ingredients:

4 large eggs
1/4 cup milk
1/2 cup diced bell peppers (any color)
1/2 cup diced onions
1/2 cup diced tomatoes
1/2 cup shredded cheddar cheese
2 slices cooked bacon, crumbled (optional)
Salt and pepper to taste
Chopped fresh parsley for garnish (optional)

Instructions:

1. In a bowl, whisk together the eggs and milk until well combined.
2. Season with salt and pepper to taste.
3. Divide the diced bell peppers, diced onions, diced tomatoes, shredded cheddar cheese, and crumbled bacon (if using) evenly among jars.
4. Pour the egg mixture over the ingredients in each jar, dividing evenly.
5. Seal the jars tightly with lids.

For Freeze-Drying:

- **Prepare**: Allow the Breakfast Scramble Jars to freeze completely.
- **Freeze**: Once frozen, remove the jars from the freezer and place them in a freeze dryer.
- **Freeze Dry**: Freeze dry the Breakfast Scramble Jars at -40°F for 24 to 48 hours until completely dry.
- **Store**: Once dry, remove the jars from the freeze dryer and store them in a cool, dry place.

Rehydrating:

- **Rehydrate**: To rehydrate, remove the lids from the jars. Add hot water to the jars, filling them to just below the rim. Stir the contents of the jars to combine the ingredients. Let the jars sit for about 10-15 minutes, stirring occasionally, until fully rehydrated and heated through.
- **Serve**: Garnish with chopped fresh parsley before serving, if desired.

Lasagna Jar

SERVINGS: 4   **PREP TIME:** 15 MIN   **COOK TIME:** 20 MIN   **FREEZE-DRY TIME:** 24-48 HRS

Ingredients:

1 cup uncooked lasagna sheets, broken into small pieces
1 cup marinara sauce
1 cup ricotta cheese
1 cup shredded mozzarella cheese
1/4 cup grated Parmesan cheese
1/2 cup diced cooked vegetables (such as bell peppers, mushrooms, or spinach)
Salt and pepper to taste
Fresh basil leaves for garnish (optional)

Instructions:

1. In a bowl, mix together the broken lasagna noodles, marinara sauce, diced cooked vegetables, salt, and pepper until well combined.
2. In jars, layer the lasagna noodle mixture, ricotta cheese, shredded mozzarella cheese, and grated Parmesan cheese, dividing evenly and creating layers.
3. Seal the jars tightly with lids.

For Freeze-Drying:

- **Prepare**: Allow the Lasagna Jars to freeze completely.
- **Freeze**: Once frozen, remove the jars from the freezer and place them in a freeze dryer.
- **Freeze Dry**: Freeze dry the Lasagna Jars at -40°F for 24 to 48 hours until completely dry.
- **Store**: Once dry, remove the jars from the freeze dryer and store them in a cool, dry place.

Rehydrating:

- **Rehydrate**: To rehydrate, remove the lids from the jars. Add hot water to the jars, filling them to just below the rim. Stir the contents of the jars to combine the ingredients. Let the jars sit for about 10-15 minutes, stirring occasionally, until fully rehydrated and heated through.
- **Serve**: Garnish with fresh basil leaves before serving, if desired.

Chapter Eight

Yummy Snacks

Apple Chips

SERVINGS: 4   **PREP TIME:** 15 MIN   **COOK TIME:** 2 HRS   **FREEZE-DRY TIME:** 24-48 HRS

Ingredients:

4 large apples (any variety)
Lemon juice (optional, to prevent browning)

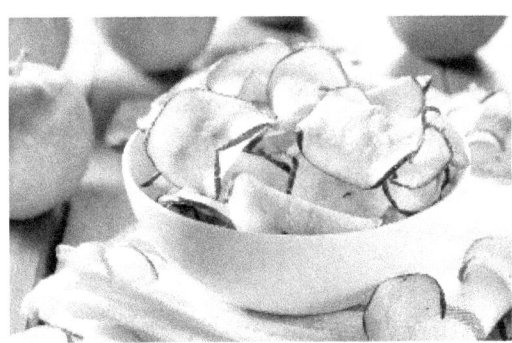

Instructions:

1. Preheat your oven to 200°F and line a baking sheet with parchment paper.
2. Wash the apples thoroughly and pat them dry with a clean towel.
3. Core the apples and slice them thinly, about 1/8 inch thick, using a sharp knife or a mandoline slicer. If desired, you can leave the peel on for added texture and nutrition.
4. Optional: To prevent the apple slices from browning, you can soak them in a bowl of water with a splash of lemon juice for a few minutes, then drain and pat dry before proceeding.
5. Arrange the apple slices in a single layer on the prepared baking sheet, making sure they are not overlapping.
6. Bake the apple slices in the preheated oven for 1.5 to 2 hours, flipping them halfway through, until they are dried and crispy. Keep an eye on them towards the end to prevent burning.
7. Once the apple chips are done, remove them from the oven and let them cool completely on the baking sheet.
8. Once cooled, store the apple chips in an airtight container at room temperature for up to a week.

For Freeze-Drying:

- **Prepare**: Place the apple chips in a single layer on a tray or baking sheet lined with parchment paper.
- **Freeze**: Place the tray in the freezer and allow the apple chips to freeze completely. Once frozen, remove the apple chips from the freezer and place them in a freeze dryer.
- **Freeze Dry**: Freeze dry the apple chips at -40°F for 24 to 48 hours until completely dry.
- **Store**: Once dry, remove the apple chips from the freeze dryer and store them in an airtight container in a cool, dry place.

Rehydrating:

- **Rehydrate**: To rehydrate, remove the desired amount from the container. Place the apple chips in a bowl and cover them with hot water. Let the apple chips soak in the hot water for about 10-15 minutes, until they become plump and rehydrated. Drain any excess water and pat the apple chips dry with a clean towel.
- **Serve**: Enjoy the rehydrated apple chips as a healthy and delicious snack.

Banana Slices

SERVINGS: 4   **PREP TIME:** 15 MIN   **COOK TIME:** 0 MIN   **FREEZE-DRY TIME:** 24-48 HRS

Ingredients:

Ripe bananas

Instructions:

1. Peel the bananas and slice them into thin rounds, about 1/4 inch thick, using a sharp knife.
2. Place the banana slices in a single layer on a baking sheet lined with parchment paper, making sure they are not overlapping.

Optional: If desired, you can dip the banana slices in lemon juice to prevent browning, although this step is not necessary.

For Freeze-Drying:

- **Prepare:** Place the baking sheet in the freezer and allow the banana slices to freeze completely, for about 1-2 hours.
- **Freeze:** Once frozen, remove the banana slices from the freezer and transfer them to a freeze dryer.
- **Freeze Dry:** Freeze dry the banana slices at -40°F for 24 to 48 hours until completely dry.
- **Store:** Once dry, remove the banana slices from the freeze dryer and let them cool to room temperature. Store the freeze-dried banana slices in an airtight container at room temperature.

Rehydrating:

- **Rehydrate:** To rehydrate, remove the desired amount from the container. Place the banana slices in a bowl and cover them with hot water. Let the banana slices soak in the hot water for about 5-10 minutes, until they become soft and plump. Drain any excess water and pat the banana slices dry with a clean towel.
- **Serve:** Enjoy the rehydrated banana slices as a snack or use them in recipes.

Berries Mix

SERVINGS: 4   **PREP TIME:** 15 MIN   **COOK TIME:** 0 MIN   **FREEZE-DRY TIME:** 12-24 HRS

Ingredients:

1 cup strawberries, washed, hulled, and sliced
1 cup blueberries, washed and dried
1 cup raspberries, washed and dried
1 cup blackberries, washed and dried

Optional: 1 tablespoon lemon juice (to prevent browning)

Instructions:

1. Prepare the berries by washing them thoroughly and drying them gently with paper towels or a clean kitchen towel.
2. If using strawberries, hull and slice them.

Optional: If you're concerned about the berries browning, you can toss them in lemon juice. Simply sprinkle the lemon juice over the berries and gently toss to coat.

For Freeze-Drying:

- **Prepare**: Spread the prepared berries in a single layer on a parchment-lined baking sheet. Make sure the berries are not touching or overlapping.
- **Freeze**: Place the baking sheet in the freezer and let the berries freeze completely, which usually takes about 1-2 hours. Once the berries are frozen solid, remove them from the freezer and transfer them to a freeze dryer.
- **Freeze Dry**: Freeze dry the berries at -40°F for 12 to 24 hours until completely dry.
- **Store**: Once the berries are freeze-dried and completely dry, remove them from the freeze dryer and let them cool to room temperature. Store the freeze-dried berries mix in an airtight container in a cool, dry place away from direct sunlight.

Rehydrating:

- **Rehydrate**: To rehydrate, remove the desired amount from the container. Place the freeze-dried berries in a bowl and cover them with hot water. The water should be just enough to cover the berries. Let the berries soak in the hot water for about 5-10 minutes, or until they become soft and plump. Drain any excess water and pat the berries dry with a clean kitchen towel.
- **Serve**: Enjoy the rehydrated berries mix as a snack, add them to cereal, yogurt, or use them in baking and desserts.

Yogurt Drops

SERVINGS: 4   **PREP TIME:** 15 MIN   **COOK TIME:** 0 MIN   **FREEZE-DRY TIME:** 12-24 HRS

Ingredients:

1 cup plain Greek yogurt
1 tablespoon honey or maple syrup (optional, for sweetness)
Fresh fruit puree or mashed ripe fruit (optional, for flavor and color)

Instructions:

1. In a mixing bowl, combine the Greek yogurt with honey or maple syrup if using.
2. Mix well until smooth and creamy.
3. If desired, add fresh fruit puree or mashed ripe fruit to the yogurt mixture for added flavor and color.
4. Mix until well combined.

For Freeze-Drying:

- **Prepare**: Line a baking sheet with parchment paper or a silicone baking mat. Use a small spoon or a piping bag to drop small dollops of the yogurt mixture onto the prepared baking sheet, spacing them evenly apart.
- **Freeze**: Place the baking sheet in the freezer and allow the yogurt drops to freeze completely, which usually takes about 1-2 hours. Once the yogurt drops are frozen solid, remove them from the freezer and transfer them to a freeze dryer.
- **Freeze Dry**: Freeze dry the yogurt drops at -40°F for 12 to 24 hours until completely dry. Once the yogurt drops are freeze-dried and completely dry, remove them from the freeze dryer and let them cool to room temperature.
- **Store**: Store the freeze-dried yogurt drops in an airtight container in a cool, dry place away from direct sunlight.

Rehydrating:

- **Rehydrate**: To rehydrate, remove the desired amount from the container. Place the freeze-dried yogurt drops in a bowl and cover them with hot water. The water should be just enough to cover the drops. Let the yogurt drops soak in the hot water for about 5-10 minutes, or until they become soft and rehydrated. Drain any excess water and pat the yogurt drops dry with a clean kitchen towel.
- **Serve**: Enjoy the rehydrated yogurt drops as a healthy snack or as a topping for yogurt, cereal, or desserts.

Sweet Potato Fries

SERVINGS: 4   **PREP TIME:** 15 MIN   **COOK TIME:** 30 MIN   **FREEZE-DRY TIME:** 24-48 HRS

Ingredients:

2 large sweet potatoes
2 tablespoons olive oil
1 teaspoon paprika
1/2 teaspoon garlic powder
1/2 teaspoon onion powder
Salt and pepper to taste

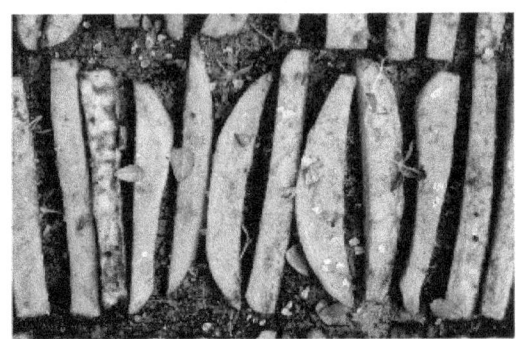

Instructions:

1. Preheat your oven to 425°F and line a baking sheet with parchment paper.
2. Wash and scrub the sweet potatoes thoroughly to remove any dirt. Peel the sweet potatoes if desired, although leaving the skin on is nutritious.
3. Cut the sweet potatoes into thin strips, about 1/4 inch wide, using a sharp knife or a mandoline slicer.
4. In a large bowl, toss the sweet potato strips with olive oil, paprika, garlic powder, onion powder, salt, and pepper until evenly coated.
5. Arrange the seasoned sweet potato strips in a single layer on the prepared baking sheet, making sure they are not overlapping.
6. Bake the sweet potato fries in the preheated oven for 20-25 minutes, flipping them halfway through, until they are golden brown and crispy.
7. Once the sweet potato fries are done, remove them from the oven and let them cool slightly before serving.

For Freeze-Drying:

- **Prepare**: Allow the Sweet Potato Fries to cool completely. Spread the cooled fries in a single layer on a tray or baking sheet lined with parchment paper.
- **Freeze**: Place the tray in the freezer and allow the fries to freeze completely. Once frozen, remove the fries from the freezer and transfer them to a freeze dryer.
- **Freeze Dry**: Freeze dry the Sweet Potato Fries at -40°F for 24 to 48 hours until completely dry.
- **Store**: Once dry, remove the fries from the freeze dryer and store them in an airtight container in a cool, dry place.

Rehydrating:

- **Rehydrate**: To rehydrate, remove the desired amount from the container. Place the fries in a bowl and cover them with hot water. Let the fries soak in the hot water for about 5-10 minutes, until they become soft and rehydrated. Drain any excess water and pat the fries dry with a clean kitchen towel. Place the rehydrated fries on a baking sheet and bake them in a preheated oven at 425°F for 5-10 minutes, until they are heated through and crispy.
- **Serve**: Serve the rehydrated Sweet Potato Fries immediately as a delicious and nutritious snack or side dish.

Cheese Cubes

SERVINGS: 4　　**PREP TIME:** 20 MIN　　**COOK TIME:** 0 MIN　　**FREEZE-DRY TIME:** 12-24 HRS

Ingredients:

8 oz block of cheese (cheddar, mozzarella, or your preferred type)

Instructions:

1. Start by selecting your favorite type of cheese and ensure it's at room temperature for easier cutting.
2. Using a sharp knife, cut the cheese block into small cubes, approximately 1/2 to 1 inch in size.
3. Arrange the cheese cubes in a single layer on a parchment-lined baking sheet, making sure they are not touching or overlapping.

For Freeze-Drying:

- **Prepare**: Place the baking sheet in the freezer and allow the cheese cubes to freeze completely, typically for about 1-2 hours.
- **Freeze**: Once the cheese cubes are frozen solid, remove them from the freezer and transfer them to a freeze dryer.
- **Freeze Dry**: Freeze dry the cheese cubes at -40°F for 24 to 48 hours until completely dry. Once the cheese cubes are freeze-dried and completely dry, remove them from the freeze dryer and let them cool to room temperature.
- **Store**: Store the freeze-dried cheese cubes in an airtight container in a cool, dry place away from direct sunlight.

Rehydrating:

- **Rehydrate**: To rehydrate, remove the desired amount from the container. Place the cheese cubes in a bowl and cover them with hot water. The water should be just enough to cover the cubes. Let the cheese cubes soak in the hot water for about 5-10 minutes, or until they become soft and plump. Drain any excess water and pat the cheese cubes dry with a clean kitchen towel.
- **Serve**: Enjoy the rehydrated cheese cubes as a snack, or use them in recipes such as salads, sandwiches, or cheese platters.

Vegetable Chips

SERVINGS: 4   **PREP TIME:** 15 MIN   **COOK TIME:** 15 MIN   **FREEZE-DRY TIME:** 24-48 HRS

Ingredients:

Assorted vegetables (such as sweet potatoes, beets, carrots, zucchini, parsnips, or kale)

Olive oil

Salt and pepper, to taste

Optional seasonings (such as garlic powder, onion powder, paprika, or herbs)

Instructions:

1. Preheat your oven to 375°F and line baking sheets with parchment paper.
2. Wash and scrub the vegetables thoroughly to remove any dirt. Peel if necessary and slice them thinly, about 1/8 inch thick, using a sharp knife or a mandoline slicer.
3. Place the sliced vegetables in a large bowl and drizzle with olive oil. Toss until the vegetables are evenly coated with oil.
4. Season the vegetables with salt, pepper, and any optional seasonings of your choice. Toss again to evenly distribute the seasonings.
5. Arrange the seasoned vegetable slices in a single layer on the prepared baking sheets, making sure they are not overlapping.
6. Bake in the preheated oven for 10-15 minutes, or until the edges of the chips are crispy and golden brown. Keep an eye on them towards the end to prevent burning.
7. Once done, remove the vegetable chips from the oven and let them cool on the baking sheets for a few minutes.

For Freeze-Drying:

- **Prepare**: Allow the Vegetable Chips to cool completely. Spread the cooled chips in a single layer on a tray or baking sheet lined with parchment paper.
- **Freeze**: Place the tray in the freezer and allow the chips to freeze completely. Once frozen, remove the chips from the freezer and transfer them to a freeze dryer.
- **Freeze Dry**: Freeze dry the Vegetable Chips at -40°F for 24 to 48 hours until completely dry.
- **Store**: Once dry, remove the chips from the freeze dryer and store them in an airtight container in a cool, dry place.

Rehydrating:

- **Rehydrate**: To rehydrate, remove the desired amount from the container. Place the chips in a bowl and cover them with hot water. The water should be just enough to cover the chips. Let the chips soak in the hot water for about 5-10 minutes, or until they become soft and rehydrated. Drain any excess water and pat the chips dry with a clean kitchen towel.
- **Serve**: Enjoy the rehydrated Vegetable Chips as a healthy and flavorful snack.

Mango Strips

SERVINGS: 4   **PREP TIME:** 15 MIN   **COOK TIME:** 15 MIN   **FREEZE-DRY TIME:** 12-24 HRS

Ingredients:

Ripe mangoes

Instructions:

1. Start by selecting ripe mangoes that are firm yet slightly soft to the touch.
2. Wash the mangoes thoroughly under running water and pat them dry with a clean kitchen towel.
3. Using a sharp knife, carefully peel the mangoes and remove the flesh from the pit.
4. Slice the mango flesh into thin strips, about 1/4 inch wide, using a sharp knife or a mandoline slicer.

For Freeze-Drying:

- **Prepare**: Arrange the mango strips in a single layer on a parchment-lined baking sheet, making sure they are not touching or overlapping.
- **Freeze**: Place the baking sheet in the freezer and allow the mango strips to freeze completely, typically for about 1-2 hours. Once the mango strips are frozen solid, remove them from the freezer and transfer them to a freeze dryer.
- **Freeze Dry**: Freeze dry the mango strips at -40°F for 12 to 24 hours until completely dry. Once the mango strips are freeze-dried and completely dry, remove them from the freeze dryer and let them cool to room temperature.
- **Store**: Store the freeze-dried mango strips in an airtight container in a cool, dry place away from direct sunlight.

Rehydrating:

- **Rehydrate**: To rehydrate, remove the desired amount from the container. Place the mango strips in a bowl and cover them with hot water. The water should be just enough to cover the strips. Let the mango strips soak in the hot water for about 5-10 minutes, or until they become soft and plump. Drain any excess water and pat the mango strips dry with a clean kitchen towel.
- **Serve**: Enjoy the rehydrated mango strips as a healthy and delicious snack, or use them in recipes such as smoothies, salads, or desserts.

Peas and Corn

SERVINGS: 4   **PREP TIME:** 15 MIN   **COOK TIME:** 5 MIN   **FREEZE-DRY TIME:** 24-48 HRS

Ingredients:

1 cup frozen peas
1 cup frozen corn kernels
Salt and pepper, to taste
1 tablespoon butter or olive oil (optional)

Instructions:

1. In a pot of boiling water, cook the frozen peas and corn for about 3-5 minutes, or until they are tender. Alternatively, you can steam them until they are cooked through.
2. Once cooked, drain the peas and corn and transfer them to a bowl.
3. Season the peas and corn with salt, pepper, and butter or olive oil if desired.
4. Toss to coat evenly.
5. Serve the peas and corn as a side dish alongside your favorite main course, or use them as ingredients in salads, soups, or casseroles.

For Freeze-Drying:

- **Prepare**: Allow the cooked Peas and Corn to cool completely. Spread the cooled peas and corn in a single layer on a tray or baking sheet lined with parchment paper.
- **Freeze**: Place the tray in the freezer and allow the peas and corn to freeze completely. Once frozen, remove the peas and corn from the freezer and transfer them to a freeze dryer.
- **Freeze Dry**: Freeze dry the Peas and Corn at -40°F for 24 to 48 hours until completely dry.
- **Store**: Once dry, remove the peas and corn from the freeze dryer and store them in an airtight container in a cool, dry place.

Rehydrating:

- **Rehydrate**: To rehydrate the freeze-dried Peas and Corn, remove the desired amount from the container. Place the peas and corn in a bowl and cover them with hot water. The water should be just enough to cover the peas and corn. Let the peas and corn soak in the hot water for about 5-10 minutes, or until they become soft and rehydrated. Drain any excess water and pat the peas and corn dry with a clean kitchen towel.
- **Serve**: Serve the rehydrated Peas and Corn as desired, either as a side dish or as ingredients in your favorite recipes.

Mixed Nuts and Seeds

SERVINGS: 4   **PREP TIME:** 15 MIN   **COOK TIME:** 15 MIN   **FREEZE-DRY TIME:** 24-48 HRS

Ingredients:

1 cup mixed nuts (such as almonds, cashews, walnuts, pecans)

1/2 cup mixed seeds (such as pumpkin seeds, sunflower seeds, flaxseeds, chia seeds)

Optional:

1-2 tablespoons maple syrup or honey

1 teaspoon cinnamon

Pinch of salt

Instructions:

1. Preheat your oven to 350°F and line a baking sheet with parchment paper.
2. In a large bowl, combine the mixed nuts and seeds.
3. If using maple syrup or honey, drizzle it over the nuts and seeds. Sprinkle with cinnamon and a pinch of salt if desired. Toss well to coat evenly.
4. Spread the nut and seed mixture in a single layer on the prepared baking sheet.
5. Bake in the preheated oven for 10-15 minutes, stirring halfway through, until the nuts are toasted and golden brown.
6. Once done, remove the baking sheet from the oven and let the mixed nuts and seeds cool completely.

For Freeze-Drying:

- **Prepare**: Allow the cooled Mixed Nuts and Seeds to cool completely. Spread the cooled nuts and seeds in a single layer on a tray or baking sheet lined with parchment paper.
- **Freeze**: Place the tray in the freezer and allow the nuts and seeds to freeze completely. Once frozen, remove the nuts and seeds from the freezer and transfer them to a freeze dryer.
- **Freeze Dry**: Freeze dry the Mixed Nuts and Seeds at -40°F for 24 to 48 hours until completely dry.
- **Store**: Once dry, remove the nuts and seeds from the freeze dryer and store them in an airtight container in a cool, dry place.

Rehydrating:

- **Rehydrate**: To rehydrate the freeze-dried Mixed Nuts and Seeds, remove the desired amount from the container. Place the nuts and seeds in a bowl and cover them with hot water. The water should be just enough to cover the nuts and seeds. Let the nuts and seeds soak in the hot water for about 5-10 minutes, or until they become soft and rehydrated. Drain any excess water and pat the nuts and seeds dry with a clean kitchen towel.
- **Serve**: Serve the rehydrated Mixed Nuts and Seeds as desired, either as a snack or as ingredients in your favorite recipes.

Chapter Nine

Desserts to Die For

Fruit Slices

SERVINGS: 4 **PREP TIME:** 15 MIN **COOK TIME:** 0 MIN **FREEZE-DRY TIME:** 12-24 HRS

Ingredients:

Assorted fruits (such as apples, pears, oranges, pineapple, strawberries, kiwi, berries, and bananas)

Instructions:

1. Start by selecting ripe and firm fruits.
2. Wash them thoroughly under running water and pat them dry with a clean kitchen towel.
3. Using a sharp knife or a mandoline slicer, slice the fruits into thin slices, about 1/4 inch thick.

For Freeze-Drying:

- **Prepare**: Arrange the fruit slices in a single layer on a parchment-lined baking sheet, making sure they are not touching or overlapping.
- **Freeze**: Place the baking sheet in the freezer and allow the fruit slices to freeze completely, typically for about 1-2 hours. Once the fruit slices are frozen solid, remove them from the freezer and transfer them to a freeze dryer.
- **Freeze Dry**: Freeze dry the fruit slices at -40°F for 12 to 24 hours until completely dry.
- **Store**: Once the fruit slices are freeze-dried and completely dry, remove them from the freeze dryer and let them cool to room temperature. Store the freeze-dried fruit slices in an airtight container in a cool, dry place away from direct sunlight.

Rehydrating:

- **Rehydrate**: To rehydrate, remove the desired amount from the container. Place the fruit slices in a bowl and cover them with hot water. The water should be just enough to cover the slices. Let the fruit slices soak in the hot water for about 5-10 minutes, or until they become soft and plump. Drain any excess water and pat the fruit slices dry with a clean kitchen towel.
- **Serve**: Enjoy the rehydrated Fruit Slices as a healthy and delicious snack, or use them in recipes such as smoothies, salads, or desserts.

Cheesecake Bites

SERVINGS: 4   **PREP TIME:** 15 MIN   **COOK TIME:** 25 MIN   **FREEZE-DRY TIME:** 24-48 HRS

Ingredients:

8 oz (225g) cream cheese, softened
1/4 cup (50g) granulated sugar
1 teaspoon vanilla extract
1 large egg
1/4 cup (60ml) sour cream
Graham cracker crumbs (optional, for coating)
Fresh berries or fruit compote, for garnish (optional)

Instructions:

1. Preheat your oven to 325°F and line a mini muffin tin with paper liners.
2. In a mixing bowl, beat the softened cream cheese and granulated sugar until smooth and creamy.
3. Add the vanilla extract and egg, and beat until well combined.
4. Stir in the sour cream until evenly incorporated into the mixture.
5. Spoon the cheesecake batter into the prepared mini muffin tin, filling each cavity almost to the top.
6. Bake in the preheated oven for 12-15 minutes, or until the cheesecake bites are set around the edges but slightly jiggly in the center.
7. Remove the cheesecake bites from the oven and let them cool in the muffin tin for about 10 minutes.
8. Transfer the cheesecake bites to a wire rack to cool completely.
9. Once cooled, optionally roll the cheesecake bites in graham cracker crumbs for added texture and flavor.
10. Garnish the cheesecake bites with fresh berries or fruit compote if desired.
11. Serve the cheesecake bites immediately, or refrigerate them until ready to serve.

For Freeze-Drying:

- **Prepare**: Allow the Cheesecake Bites to cool completely. Arrange the cooled cheesecake bites in a single layer on a tray or baking sheet lined with parchment paper.
- **Freeze**: Place the tray in the freezer and allow the cheesecake bites to freeze completely. Once frozen, remove the cheesecake bites from the freezer and transfer them to a freeze dryer.
- **Freeze Dry**: Freeze dry the Cheesecake Bites at -40°F for 24 to 48 hours until completely dry.
- **Store**: Once dry, remove the cheesecake bites from the freeze dryer and let them cool to room temperature. Store the freeze-dried cheesecake bites in an airtight container in a cool, dry place.

Rehydrating:

- **Rehydrate**: To rehydrate, remove the desired amount from the container. Place the cheesecake bites in a bowl and cover them with hot water. The water should be just enough to cover the bites. Let the cheesecake bites soak in the hot water for about 5-10 minutes, or until they become soft and rehydrated. Drain any excess water and pat the cheesecake bites dry with a clean kitchen towel.
- **Serve**: Serve the rehydrated Cheesecake Bites as desired, either as a dessert on their own or as part of a larger dish.

Chocolate-Covered Berries

SERVINGS: 4   **PREP TIME:** 25 MIN   **COOK TIME:** 5 MIN   **FREEZE-DRY TIME:** 24-48 HRS

Ingredients:

Fresh strawberries, raspberries, or blueberries
Dark, milk, or white chocolate chips or bars

Optional:

Coconut oil, for thinning the chocolate
Chopped nuts, shredded coconut, or sprinkles for topping

Instructions:

1. Rinse the berries under cold water and pat them dry with a paper towel. Make sure they are completely dry to prevent the chocolate from seizing.
2. Line a baking sheet with parchment paper or wax paper.
3. In a microwave-safe bowl, melt the chocolate chips or bars in 30-second intervals, stirring between each interval until smooth and fully melted. If desired, add a teaspoon of coconut oil to the chocolate to help thin it out for easier dipping.
4. Using a toothpick or skewer, dip each berry into the melted chocolate, coating it halfway or fully, depending on your preference.
5. Gently shake off any excess chocolate and place the dipped berries onto the prepared baking sheet.
6. If desired, sprinkle chopped nuts, shredded coconut, or sprinkles over the chocolate-covered berries before the chocolate sets.
7. Once all the berries are dipped, place the baking sheet in the refrigerator for about 15-20 minutes, or until the chocolate has hardened.

For Freeze-Drying:

- **Prepare**: Allow the Chocolate-Covered Berries to cool completely. Arrange the cooled berries in a single layer on a tray or baking sheet lined with parchment paper.
- **Freeze**: Place the tray in the freezer and allow the berries to freeze completely. Once frozen, remove the berries from the freezer and transfer them to a freeze dryer.
- **Freeze Dry**: Freeze dry the Chocolate-Covered Berries at -40°F for 24 to 48 hours until completely dry. Once dry, remove the berries from the freeze dryer and let them cool to room temperature.
- **Store**: Store the freeze-dried Chocolate-Covered Berries in an airtight container in a cool, dry place.

Rehydrating:

- **Rehydrate**: To rehydrate, remove the desired amount from the container. Place the berries in a bowl and cover them with hot water. The water should be just enough to cover the berries. Let the berries soak in the hot water for about 5-10 minutes, or until they become soft and rehydrated. Drain any excess water and pat the berries dry with a clean kitchen towel.
- **Serve**: Serve the rehydrated Chocolate-Covered Berries as desired, either as a decadent dessert or as a topping for cakes, ice cream, or yogurt.

Marshmallows

SERVINGS: 4   **PREP TIME:** 4 HRS   **COOK TIME:** 25 MIN   **FREEZE-DRY TIME:** 24-48 HRS

Ingredients:

3 tablespoons (3 packets) unflavored gelatin
1/2 cup cold water, divided
2 cups granulated sugar
1/2 cup light corn syrup
1/4 teaspoon salt
2 teaspoons vanilla extract
Powdered sugar, for dusting

Instructions:

1. In a large mixing bowl, sprinkle the gelatin over 1/4 cup of cold water. Let it sit for about 10 minutes to soften.
2. In a small saucepan, combine the remaining 1/4 cup of water, granulated sugar, corn syrup, and salt. Stir over medium heat until the sugar has dissolved.
3. Increase the heat to medium-high and bring the mixture to a boil without stirring. Insert a candy thermometer and continue boiling until the mixture reaches 240°F, which is the soft-ball stage.
4. Once the syrup reaches the desired temperature, remove it from the heat immediately.
5. With a stand mixer fitted with the whisk attachment, begin to whip the gelatin mixture on low speed. Gradually pour the hot syrup into the bowl in a slow, steady stream, avoiding the whisk to prevent splattering.
6. Increase the mixer speed to high and continue whipping until the mixture becomes thick, fluffy, and triples in volume, about 10-15 minutes.
7. Add the vanilla extract and beat for an additional minute to incorporate.
8. Lightly grease a 9x13-inch baking dish with cooking spray and dust it with powdered sugar to prevent sticking.
9. Pour the marshmallow mixture into the prepared pan, spreading it evenly with a spatula.
10. Allow the marshmallows to set at room temperature for at least 4 hours or overnight until firm and set.
11. Once set, use a sharp knife or cookie cutters dusted with powdered sugar to cut the marshmallows into squares or shapes as desired.
12. Dust the cut marshmallows with additional powdered sugar to prevent sticking.

For Freeze-Drying:

- **Prepare:** Allow the Marshmallows to set completely and firm up. Carefully remove the cut marshmallows from the baking dish and arrange them in a single layer on a tray or baking sheet lined with parchment paper.
- **Freeze:** Place the tray in the freezer and allow the marshmallows to freeze completely. Once frozen, remove the marshmallows from the freezer and transfer them to a freeze dryer.
- **Freeze Dry:** Freeze dry the Marshmallows at -40°F for 24 to 48 hours until completely dry. Once dry, remove the marshmallows from the freeze dryer and let them cool to room temperature.
- **Store:** Store the freeze-dried Marshmallows in an airtight container in a cool, dry place.

Rehydrating:

- **Rehydrate:** To rehydrate, remove the desired amount from the container. Place the marshmallows in a bowl and cover them with hot water. The water should be just enough to cover the marshmallows. Let the marshmallows soak in the hot water for about 5-10 minutes, or until they become soft and rehydrated. Drain any excess water and pat the marshmallows dry with a clean kitchen towel.
- **Serve:** Serve the rehydrated Marshmallows as desired, either as a sweet treat on their own or as a topping for hot chocolate, s'mores, or desserts.

Cookie Dough Balls

SERVINGS: 4   **PREP TIME:** 15 MIN   **COOK TIME:** 25 MIN   **FREEZE-DRY TIME:** 24-48 HRS

Ingredients:

1/2 cup (115g) unsalted butter, softened
1/2 cup (100g) packed brown sugar
1/4 cup (50g) granulated sugar
1 teaspoon vanilla extract
1 cup (125g) all-purpose flour
1/4 teaspoon salt
1/2 cup (90g) mini chocolate chips

Instructions:

1. In a mixing bowl, cream together the softened butter, brown sugar, and granulated sugar until light and fluffy.
2. Add the vanilla extract and mix until well combined.
3. Gradually add the flour and salt to the butter mixture, mixing until a dough forms.
4. Fold in the mini chocolate chips until evenly distributed throughout the dough.
5. Using a small cookie scoop or your hands, roll the dough into balls, about 1 tablespoon of dough for each ball.
6. Place the cookie dough balls on a parchment-lined baking sheet and chill in the refrigerator for at least 30 minutes to firm up.

For Freeze-Drying:

- **Prepare:** Allow the Cookie Dough Balls to chill completely. Arrange the chilled cookie dough balls in a single layer on a tray or baking sheet lined with parchment paper.
- **Freeze:** Place the tray in the freezer and allow the cookie dough balls to freeze completely. Once frozen, remove the cookie dough balls from the freezer and transfer them to a freeze dryer.
- **Freeze Dry:** Freeze dry the Cookie Dough Balls at -40°F for 24 to 48 hours until completely dry. Once dry, remove the cookie dough balls from the freeze dryer and let them cool to room temperature.
- **Store:** Store the freeze-dried Cookie Dough Balls in an airtight container in a cool, dry place.

Rehydrating:

- **Rehydrate:** To rehydrate, remove the desired amount from the container. Place the cookie dough balls in a bowl and cover them with hot water. The water should be just enough to cover the balls. Let the cookie dough balls soak in the hot water for about 5-10 minutes, or until they become soft and pliable. Drain any excess water and pat the cookie dough balls dry with a clean kitchen towel.
- **Serve:** Serve the rehydrated Cookie Dough Balls as desired, either as a sweet treat on their own or as a topping for ice cream, yogurt, or baked goods.

Candied Citrus Peels

SERVINGS: 4 **PREP TIME:** 15 MIN **COOK TIME:** 75 MIN **FREEZE-DRY TIME:** 24-48 HRS

Ingredients:

2 large oranges or lemons
2 cups granulated sugar, plus extra for coating
Water

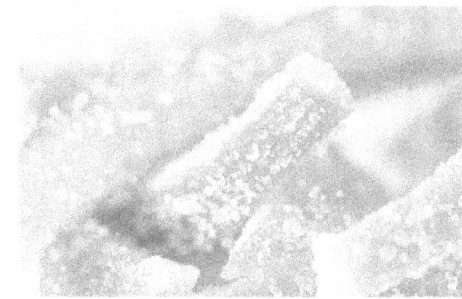

Instructions:

1. Wash the oranges or lemons thoroughly under cold water. Slice them thinly, about 1/8 inch thick, removing any seeds.
2. In a large saucepan, combine 2 cups of sugar with 2 cups of water. Stir over medium heat until the sugar has dissolved completely.
3. Add the sliced citrus to the sugar syrup in the saucepan, making sure they are submerged in the syrup.
4. Bring the mixture to a simmer over medium-low heat. Let the citrus slices simmer gently for about 45-60 minutes, or until they become translucent and slightly candied.
5. Remove the saucepan from the heat and let the candied citrus slices cool in the syrup for about 10-15 minutes.
6. Use a slotted spoon to transfer the candied citrus slices to a wire rack set over a baking sheet, allowing any excess syrup to drip off.
7. Place the wire rack in a cool, dry place and let the candied citrus slices dry for about 12-24 hours, or until they become tacky to the touch.
8. Once the candied citrus slices are tacky, roll them in granulated sugar to coat them evenly. Shake off any excess sugar and transfer the candied citrus slices to an airtight container.

For Freeze-Drying:

- **Prepare**: Allow the Candied Citrus Peels to cool completely and dry for 24 hours. Arrange the candied citrus slices in a single layer on a tray or baking sheet lined with parchment paper.
- **Freeze**: Place the tray in the freezer and allow the candied citrus slices to freeze completely. Once frozen, remove the candied citrus slices from the freezer and transfer them to a freeze dryer.
- **Freeze Dry**: Freeze dry the Candied Citrus Peels at -40°F for 24 to 48 hours until completely dry. Once dry, remove the candied citrus slices from the freeze dryer and let them cool to room temperature.
- **Store**: Store the freeze-dried Candied Citrus Peels in an airtight container in a cool, dry place.

Rehydrating:

- **Rehydrate**: To rehydrate, remove the desired amount from the container. Place the candied citrus slices in a bowl and cover them with hot water. The water should be just enough to cover the slices. Let the candied citrus slices soak in the hot water for about 5-10 minutes, or until they become soft and rehydrated. Drain any excess water and pat the candied citrus slices dry with a clean kitchen towel.
- **Serve**: Serve the rehydrated Candied Citrus Peels as desired, either as a sweet treat on their own or as a garnish for desserts, cocktails, or baked goods.

Brownie Chunks

SERVINGS: 4   **PREP TIME:** 15 MIN   **COOK TIME:** 25 MIN   **FREEZE-DRY TIME:** 24-48 HRS

Ingredients:

1/2 cup (115g) unsalted butter
1 cup (200g) granulated sugar
2 large eggs
1 teaspoon vanilla extract
1/3 cup (40g) unsweetened cocoa powder
1/2 cup (65g) all-purpose flour
1/4 teaspoon salt
1/4 teaspoon baking powder

Optional: Chocolate chips, chopped nuts, or other mix-ins of your choice

Instructions:

1. Preheat your oven to 350°F and grease a 9x9-inch baking pan.
2. In a microwave-safe bowl, melt the butter in the microwave in 30-second intervals until completely melted.
3. Stir in the granulated sugar until well combined.
4. Add the eggs, one at a time, mixing well after each addition.
5. Stir in the vanilla extract until evenly incorporated.
6. In a separate bowl, sift together the cocoa powder, flour, salt, and baking powder.
7. Gradually add the dry ingredients to the wet ingredients, mixing until just combined.
8. Fold in any optional mix-ins, such as chocolate chips or chopped nuts, if desired.
9. Pour the brownie batter into the prepared baking pan, spreading it evenly with a spatula.
10. Bake in the preheated oven for 20-25 minutes, or until a toothpick inserted into the center comes out with a few moist crumbs.
11. Remove the brownies from the oven and let them cool completely in the pan before cutting them into small, bite-sized chunks.

For Freeze-Drying:

- **Prepare**: Allow the Brownie Chunks to cool completely. Arrange the cooled brownie chunks in a single layer on a tray or baking sheet lined with parchment paper.
- **Freeze**: Place the tray in the freezer and allow the brownie chunks to freeze completely. Once frozen, remove the brownie chunks from the freezer and transfer them to a freeze dryer.
- **Freeze Dry**: Freeze dry the Brownie Chunks at -40°F for 24 to 48 hours until completely dry. Once dry, remove the brownie chunks from the freeze dryer and let them cool to room temperature.
- **Store**: Store the freeze-dried Brownie Chunks in an airtight container in a cool, dry place.

Rehydrating:

- **Rehydrate**: To rehydrate, remove the desired amount from the container. Place the brownie chunks in a bowl and cover them with hot water. The water should be just enough to cover the chunks. Let the brownie chunks soak in the hot water for about 5-10 minutes, or until they become soft and rehydrated. Drain any excess water and pat the brownie chunks dry with a clean kitchen towel.
- **Serve**: Serve the rehydrated Brownie Chunks as desired, either as a decadent dessert on their own or as a topping for ice cream, yogurt, or baked goods.

Meringue Kisses

SERVINGS: 4   **PREP TIME:** 20 MIN   **COOK TIME:** 2 HRS   **FREEZE-DRY TIME:** 24-48 HRS

Ingredients:

3 large egg whites, at room temperature
3/4 cup (150g) granulated sugar
1/4 teaspoon cream of tartar
1/2 teaspoon vanilla extract
Gel food coloring (optional)

Instructions:

1. Preheat your oven to 200°F. Line a baking sheet with parchment paper or a silicone baking mat.
2. In a clean, dry mixing bowl, beat the egg whites on medium speed until foamy.
3. Add the cream of tartar and continue to beat until soft peaks form.
4. Gradually add the granulated sugar, a tablespoon at a time, while continuing to beat the egg whites. Beat until stiff, glossy peaks form and the sugar is completely dissolved.
5. Beat in the vanilla extract until evenly incorporated.
6. If using gel food coloring, add a small amount to the meringue mixture and gently fold it in until desired color is achieved.
7. Transfer the meringue mixture to a piping bag fitted with a large star tip, or simply use a spoon to dollop small mounds of meringue onto the prepared baking sheet.
8. Pipe or spoon the meringue into small kisses or swirls, leaving a little space between each.
9. Bake the meringue kisses in the preheated oven for 1.5 to 2 hours, or until they are dry to the touch and easily lift off the parchment paper.
10. Turn off the oven and leave the meringue kisses inside to cool completely with the oven door closed.

For Freeze-Drying:

- **Prepare**: Allow the Meringue Kisses to cool completely. Arrange the cooled meringue kisses in a single layer on a tray or baking sheet lined with parchment paper.
- **Freeze**: Place the tray in the freezer and allow the meringue kisses to freeze completely. Once frozen, remove the meringue kisses from the freezer and transfer them to a freeze dryer.
- **Freeze Dry**: Freeze dry the Meringue Kisses at -40°F for 24 to 48 hours until completely dry. Once dry, remove the meringue kisses from the freeze dryer and let them cool to room temperature.
- **Store**: Store the freeze-dried Meringue Kisses in an airtight container in a cool, dry place.

Rehydrating:

- **Rehydrate**: To rehydrate, remove the desired amount from the container. Place the meringue kisses in a bowl and cover them with hot water. The water should be just enough to cover the kisses. Let the meringue kisses soak in the hot water for about 5-10 minutes, or until they become soft and rehydrated. Drain any excess water and pat the meringue kisses dry with a clean kitchen towel.
- **Serve**: Serve the rehydrated Meringue Kisses as desired, either as a light and airy treat on their own or as a topping for desserts like pies, cakes, or ice cream.

Fruit and Yogurt Parfaits

SERVINGS: 4   **PREP TIME:** 20 MIN   **COOK TIME:** 0 MIN   **FREEZE-DRY TIME:** 24-48 HRS

Ingredients:

2 cups plain Greek yogurt
2 tablespoons honey or maple syrup
1 teaspoon vanilla extract
1 cup mixed fresh fruits (such as berries, diced peaches, or chopped pineapple)
1/2 cup granola or chopped nuts
Optional: Drizzle of honey or maple syrup for serving

Instructions:

1. In a mixing bowl, combine the Greek yogurt, honey or maple syrup, and vanilla extract. Stir until smooth and well combined.
2. Prepare your serving glasses or jars. Begin layering the ingredients by spooning a dollop of the yogurt mixture into the bottom of each glass.
3. Add a layer of mixed fresh fruits on top of the yogurt layer.
4. Sprinkle a layer of granola or chopped nuts over the fruit layer.
5. Repeat the layers until the glasses are filled, ending with a layer of yogurt on top.
6. If desired, drizzle a little honey or maple syrup over the top layer of yogurt for extra sweetness.
7. Serve the fruit and yogurt parfaits immediately, or cover and refrigerate until ready to serve.

For Freeze-Drying:

- **Prepare:** Allow the Fruit and Yogurt Parfaits to chill in the refrigerator until firm. Carefully transfer the parfaits to a tray or baking sheet lined with parchment paper.
- **Freeze:** Place the tray in the freezer and allow the parfaits to freeze completely. Once frozen, remove the parfaits from the freezer and transfer them to a freeze dryer.
- **Freeze Dry:** Freeze dry the Fruit and Yogurt Parfaits at -40°F for 24 to 48 hours until completely dry. Once dry, remove the parfaits from the freeze dryer and let them cool to room temperature.
- **Store:** Store the freeze-dried Fruit and Yogurt Parfaits in an airtight container in a cool, dry place.

Rehydrating:

- **Rehydrate:** To rehydrate, remove the desired amount from the container. Place the parfaits in a bowl and cover them with hot water. The water should be just enough to cover the parfaits. Let the parfaits soak in the hot water for about 5-10 minutes, or until they become soft and rehydrated. Drain any excess water and gently stir the parfaits to distribute the yogurt and fruit evenly.
- **Serve:** Serve the rehydrated Fruit and Yogurt Parfaits immediately, enjoying the creamy yogurt, juicy fruit, and crunchy granola just like when they were freshly made.

Apple Cinnamon Chips

SERVINGS: 4   **PREP TIME:** 20 MIN   **COOK TIME:** 2 HRS   **FREEZE-DRY TIME:** 24-48 HRS

Ingredients:

2 large apples (such as Honeycrisp or Granny Smith)
1 tablespoon ground cinnamon

Optional: 1-2 tablespoons granulated sugar or brown sugar for added sweetness

Instructions:

1. Preheat your oven to 200°F and line a baking sheet with parchment paper.
2. Wash and dry the apples thoroughly. Use a sharp knife or a mandoline slicer to thinly slice the apples crosswise, about 1/8 inch thick.
3. In a small bowl, mix together the ground cinnamon and sugar, if using.
4. Arrange the apple slices in a single layer on the prepared baking sheet, making sure they do not overlap.
5. Sprinkle the cinnamon sugar mixture evenly over the apple slices, or simply sprinkle ground cinnamon over the slices for a sugar-free option.
6. Bake the apple slices in the preheated oven for 1.5 to 2 hours, or until they are dry to the touch and slightly crisp.
7. Remove the baking sheet from the oven and let the apple chips cool completely on the baking sheet before serving or storing.

For Freeze-Drying:

- **Prepare**: Allow the Apple Cinnamon Chips to cool completely. Arrange the cooled apple chips in a single layer on a tray or baking sheet lined with parchment paper.
- **Freeze**: Place the tray in the freezer and allow the apple chips to freeze completely. Once frozen, remove the apple chips from the freezer and transfer them to a freeze dryer.
- **Freeze Dry**: Freeze dry the Apple Cinnamon Chips at -40°F for 24 to 48 hours until completely dry. Once dry, remove the apple chips from the freeze dryer and let them cool to room temperature.
- **Store**: Store the freeze-dried Apple Cinnamon Chips in an airtight container in a cool, dry place.

Rehydrating:

- **Rehydrate**: To rehydrate, remove the desired amount from the container. Place the apple chips in a bowl and cover them with hot water. The water should be just enough to cover the chips. Let the apple chips soak in the hot water for about 5-10 minutes, or until they become soft and rehydrated. Drain any excess water and pat the apple chips dry with a clean kitchen towel.
- **Serve**: Serve the rehydrated Apple Cinnamon Chips immediately, enjoying the sweet and spicy flavor of cinnamon-infused apple slices.

Chapter Ten

Can't Do Without Candy

Gummy Bears

SERVINGS: 4   **PREP TIME:** 2 HRS   **COOK TIME:** 15 MIN   **FREEZE-DRY TIME:** 24-48 HRS

Ingredients:

1/2 cup fruit juice (such as orange, apple, or grape)
1/4 cup water
3 tablespoons unflavored gelatin powder
2-3 tablespoons honey or maple syrup (adjust to taste)

Optional: Food coloring, fruit puree, or flavored extracts for additional flavor and color

Instructions:

1. In a small saucepan, combine the fruit juice and water. Heat the mixture over low heat until it is warm but not boiling.
2. Gradually sprinkle the gelatin powder over the warm liquid, whisking constantly to prevent lumps from forming.
3. Continue whisking until the gelatin is completely dissolved and the mixture is smooth.
4. Stir in the honey or maple syrup until it is fully incorporated. Taste the mixture and adjust the sweetness if necessary.
5. If using, add a few drops of food coloring, fruit puree, or flavored extracts to the mixture to enhance the flavor and color of the gummy bears. Mix well.
6. Remove the saucepan from the heat and let the mixture cool slightly, but not set.
7. Pour the warm liquid into gummy bear molds using a dropper or spoon. Fill each mold cavity to the top.
8. Gently tap the molds on the countertop to remove any air bubbles and ensure the mixture settles evenly.
9. Place the filled molds in the refrigerator and let them chill for at least 1-2 hours, or until the gummy bears are set and firm to the touch.
10. Once set, carefully pop the gummy bears out of the molds and place them on a parchment-lined baking sheet.

For Freeze-Drying:

- **Prepare**: Allow the Homemade Gummy Bears to cool completely and firm up on the baking sheet. Arrange the cooled gummy bears in a single layer on a tray or baking sheet lined with parchment paper.
- **Freeze**: Place the tray in the freezer and allow the gummy bears to freeze completely. Once frozen, remove the gummy bears from the freezer and transfer them to a freeze dryer.
- **Freeze Dry**: Freeze dry the Gummy Bears at -40°F for 24 to 48 hours until completely dry. Once dry, remove the gummy bears from the freeze dryer and let them cool to room temperature.
- **Store**: Store the freeze-dried Gummy Bears in an airtight container in a cool, dry place.

Rehydrating:

- **Rehydrate**: To rehydrate, remove the desired amount from the container. Place the gummy bears in a bowl and cover them with hot water. The water should be just enough to cover the gummy bears. Let the gummy bears soak in the hot water for about 5-10 minutes, or until they become soft and rehydrated. Drain any excess water and pat the gummy bears dry with a clean kitchen towel.
- **Serve**: Serve the rehydrated Gummy Bears immediately, enjoying their chewy texture and fruity flavor.

Chocolate-Covered Strawberries

SERVINGS: 4   **PREP TIME:** 15 MIN   **COOK TIME:** 5 MIN   **FREEZE-DRY TIME:** 24-48 HRS

Ingredients:

Fresh strawberries, washed and dried
Dark, milk, or white chocolate chips or bars

Optional: Decorative toppings such as chopped nuts, sprinkles, or coconut flakes

Instructions:

1. Line a baking sheet with parchment paper or wax paper and set it aside.
2. In a heatproof bowl, melt the chocolate chips or bars in the microwave in 30-second intervals, stirring between each interval until smooth and fully melted. Alternatively, you can melt the chocolate using a double boiler on the stovetop.
3. Hold each strawberry by the stem and dip it into the melted chocolate, swirling to coat it evenly. Allow any excess chocolate to drip off.
4. If desired, roll the chocolate-covered strawberry in your choice of decorative toppings while the chocolate is still wet.
5. Place the chocolate-covered strawberries onto the prepared baking sheet, making sure they are not touching each other.
6. Once all the strawberries are coated, place the baking sheet in the refrigerator for about 30 minutes to allow the chocolate to set and harden.
7. Once the chocolate has hardened, the chocolate-covered strawberries are ready to serve or store. Enjoy them as a delicious treat or dessert!

For Freeze-Drying:

- **Prepare**: Allow the Chocolate-Covered Strawberries to cool completely and firm up on the baking sheet. Arrange the cooled chocolate-covered strawberries in a single layer on a tray or baking sheet lined with parchment paper.
- **Freeze**: Place the tray in the freezer and allow the chocolate-covered strawberries to freeze completely. Once frozen, remove the chocolate-covered strawberries from the freezer and transfer them to a freeze dryer.
- **Freeze Dry**: Freeze dry the Chocolate-Covered Strawberries at -40°F for 24 to 48 hours until completely dry. Once dry, remove the chocolate-covered strawberries from the freeze dryer and let them cool to room temperature.
- **Store**: Store the freeze-dried Chocolate-Covered Strawberries in an airtight container in a cool, dry place.

Rehydrating:

- **Rehydrate**: To rehydrate, remove the desired amount from the container. Place the chocolate-covered strawberries in a bowl and cover them with hot water. The water should be just enough to cover the strawberries. Let the chocolate-covered strawberries soak in the hot water for about 5-10 minutes, or until they become soft and rehydrated. Drain any excess water and pat the chocolate-covered strawberries dry with a clean kitchen towel.
- **Serve**: Serve the rehydrated Chocolate-Covered Strawberries immediately, enjoying the combination of juicy strawberries and rich chocolate.

Marshmallows

SERVINGS: 4   **PREP TIME:** 4 HRS   **COOK TIME:** 25 MIN   **FREEZE-DRY TIME:** 24-48 HRS

Ingredients:

3 tablespoons (3 packets) unflavored gelatin
1/2 cup cold water, divided
2 cups granulated sugar
1/2 cup light corn syrup
1/4 teaspoon salt
2 teaspoons vanilla extract
Powdered sugar, for dusting

Instructions:

1. In a large mixing bowl, sprinkle the gelatin over 1/4 cup of cold water. Let it sit for about 10 minutes to soften.
2. In a small saucepan, combine the remaining 1/4 cup of water, granulated sugar, corn syrup, and salt. Stir over medium heat until the sugar has dissolved.
3. Increase the heat to medium-high and bring the mixture to a boil without stirring. Insert a candy thermometer and continue boiling until the mixture reaches 240°F, which is the soft-ball stage.
4. Once the syrup reaches the desired temperature, remove it from the heat immediately.
5. With a stand mixer fitted with the whisk attachment, begin to whip the gelatin mixture on low speed. Gradually pour the hot syrup into the bowl in a slow, steady stream, avoiding the whisk to prevent splattering.
6. Increase the mixer speed to high and continue whipping until the mixture becomes thick, fluffy, and triples in volume, about 10-15 minutes.
7. Add the vanilla extract and beat for an additional minute to incorporate.
8. Lightly grease a 9x13-inch baking dish with cooking spray and dust it with powdered sugar to prevent sticking.
9. Pour the marshmallow mixture into the prepared pan, spreading it evenly with a spatula.
10. Allow the marshmallows to set at room temperature for at least 4 hours or overnight until firm and set.
11. Once set, use a sharp knife or cookie cutters dusted with powdered sugar to cut the marshmallows into squares or shapes as desired.
12. Dust the cut marshmallows with additional powdered sugar to prevent sticking.

For Freeze-Drying:

- **Prepare**: Allow the Marshmallows to set completely and firm up. Carefully remove the cut marshmallows from the baking dish and arrange them in a single layer on a tray or baking sheet lined with parchment paper.
- **Freeze**: Place the tray in the freezer and allow the marshmallows to freeze completely. Once frozen, remove the marshmallows from the freezer and transfer them to a freeze dryer.
- **Freeze Dry**: Freeze dry the Marshmallows at -40°F for 24 to 48 hours until completely dry. Once dry, remove the marshmallows from the freeze dryer and let them cool to room temperature.
- **Store**: Store the freeze-dried Marshmallows in an airtight container in a cool, dry place.

Rehydrating:

- **Rehydrate**: To rehydrate, remove the desired amount from the container. Place the marshmallows in a bowl and cover them with hot water. The water should be just enough to cover the marshmallows. Let the marshmallows soak in the hot water for about 5-10 minutes, or until they become soft and rehydrated. Drain any excess water and pat the marshmallows dry with a clean kitchen towel.
- **Serve**: Serve the rehydrated Marshmallows as desired, either as a sweet treat on their own or as a topping for hot chocolate, s'mores, or desserts.

Sour Candy Strips

SERVINGS: 4   **PREP TIME:** 20 MIN   **COOK TIME:** 25 MIN   **FREEZE-DRY TIME:** 24-48 HRS

Ingredients:

1 cup granulated sugar
1/2 cup water
1/3 cup corn syrup
1/4 cup lemon juice
1/4 cup lime juice
1/4 teaspoon citric acid (optional, for extra sourness)
Food coloring (optional)
Powdered sugar, for dusting

Instructions:

1. In a small saucepan, combine the granulated sugar, water, and corn syrup. Heat the mixture over medium heat, stirring constantly, until the sugar has dissolved.
2. Once the sugar has dissolved, bring the mixture to a boil without stirring. Insert a candy thermometer and continue to boil until the temperature reaches 300°F, which is the hard crack stage.
3. Remove the saucepan from the heat and carefully stir in the lemon juice, lime juice, and citric acid (if using). Be cautious as the mixture will bubble up.
4. If desired, add a few drops of food coloring to the mixture and stir until well combined.
5. Pour the hot candy mixture onto a parchment-lined baking sheet, spreading it out into a thin layer with a spatula.
6. Let the candy mixture cool for a few minutes until it begins to set, but is still pliable.
7. Using a sharp knife or pizza cutter, cut the candy into thin strips or squares.
8. Dust the cut candy strips with powdered sugar to prevent sticking.

For Freeze-Drying:

- **Prepare:** Allow the Sour Candy Strips to cool completely and firm up on the baking sheet. Once set, carefully remove the candy strips from the baking sheet and transfer them to a tray or baking sheet lined with parchment paper.
- **Freeze:** Place the tray in the freezer and allow the candy strips to freeze completely. Once frozen, remove the candy strips from the freezer and transfer them to a freeze dryer.
- **Freeze Dry:** Freeze dry the Sour Candy Strips at -40°F for 24 to 48 hours until completely dry. Once dry, remove the freeze-dried Sour Candy Strips from the freeze dryer and let them cool to room temperature.
- **Store:** Store the freeze-dried Sour Candy Strips in an airtight container in a cool, dry place.

Rehydrating:

- **Rehydrate:** To rehydrate, remove the desired amount from the container. Place the candy strips in a bowl and cover them with hot water. The water should be just enough to cover the candy strips. Let the candy strips soak in the hot water for about 5-10 minutes, or until they become soft and rehydrated. Drain any excess water and pat the candy strips dry with a clean kitchen towel.
- **Serve:** Serve the rehydrated Sour Candy Strips immediately, enjoying their tangy and sweet flavor.

Hard Candy

SERVINGS: 4   **PREP TIME:** 15 MIN   **COOK TIME:** 25 MIN   **FREEZE-DRY TIME:** 24-48 HRS

Ingredients:

2 cups granulated sugar
3/4 cup light corn syrup
1/2 cup water
Powdered sugar, for dusting

Optional:
Flavored extracts (such as peppermint, lemon, or cherry)
Food coloring

Instructions:

1. In a medium saucepan, combine the granulated sugar, light corn syrup, and water. Stir the mixture over medium heat until the sugar dissolves.
2. Once the sugar has dissolved, insert a candy thermometer into the saucepan and bring the mixture to a boil without stirring.
3. Continue to boil the mixture until it reaches the hard crack stage, which is around 300°F on the candy thermometer. This usually takes about 10-15 minutes.
4. Once the mixture reaches the desired temperature, remove the saucepan from the heat.
5. If using, stir in a few drops of food coloring and flavored extract to the mixture until well combined.
6. Carefully pour the hot candy mixture onto a parchment-lined baking sheet, spreading it out into an even layer with a spatula.
7. Let the candy mixture cool for a few minutes until it begins to set, but is still pliable.
8. Using a sharp knife or pizza cutter, score the candy into desired shapes or break it into pieces once it has cooled completely.
9. Dust the cut candy pieces with powdered sugar to prevent sticking.

For Freeze-Drying:

- **Prepare:** Allow the Hard Candy to cool completely and harden on the baking sheet. Once set, carefully remove the candy pieces from the baking sheet and transfer them to a tray or baking sheet lined with parchment paper.
- **Freeze:** Place the tray in the freezer and allow the hard candy pieces to freeze completely. Once frozen, remove the hard candy pieces from the freezer and transfer them to a freeze dryer.
- **Freeze Dry:** Freeze dry the Hard Candy at -40°F for 24 to 48 hours until completely dry. Once dry, remove the freeze-dried Hard Candy from the freeze dryer and let them cool to room temperature.
- **Store:** Store the freeze-dried Hard Candy in an airtight container in a cool, dry place.

Rehydrating:

- **Rehydrate:** To rehydrate, remove the desired amount from the container. Place the hard candy pieces in a bowl and cover them with hot water. The water should be just enough to cover the candy pieces. Let the hard candy pieces soak in the hot water for about 5-10 minutes, or until they become soft and rehydrated. Drain any excess water and pat the hard candy pieces dry with a clean kitchen towel.
- **Serve:** Serve the rehydrated Hard Candy immediately, enjoying their sweet and crunchy texture.

Candied Citrus Peels

SERVINGS: 4   **PREP TIME:** 15 MIN   **COOK TIME:** 75 MIN   **FREEZE-DRY TIME:** 24-48 HRS

Ingredients:

2 large oranges or lemons
2 cups granulated sugar, plus extra for coating
Water

Instructions:

1. Wash the oranges or lemons thoroughly under cold water. Slice them thinly, about 1/8 inch thick, removing any seeds.
2. In a large saucepan, combine 2 cups of sugar with 2 cups of water. Stir over medium heat until the sugar has dissolved completely.
3. Add the sliced citrus to the sugar syrup in the saucepan, making sure they are submerged in the syrup.
4. Bring the mixture to a simmer over medium-low heat. Let the citrus slices simmer gently for about 45-60 minutes, or until they become translucent and slightly candied.
5. Remove the saucepan from the heat and let the candied citrus slices cool in the syrup for about 10-15 minutes.
6. Use a slotted spoon to transfer the candied citrus slices to a wire rack set over a baking sheet, allowing any excess syrup to drip off.
7. Place the wire rack in a cool, dry place and let the candied citrus slices dry for about 12-24 hours, or until they become tacky to the touch.
8. Once the candied citrus slices are tacky, roll them in granulated sugar to coat them evenly. Shake off any excess sugar and transfer the candied citrus slices to an airtight container.

For Freeze-Drying:

- **Prepare**: Allow the Candied Citrus Peels to cool completely and dry for 24 hours. Arrange the candied citrus slices in a single layer on a tray or baking sheet lined with parchment paper.
- **Freeze**: Place the tray in the freezer and allow the candied citrus slices to freeze completely. Once frozen, remove the candied citrus slices from the freezer and transfer them to a freeze dryer.
- **Freeze Dry**: Freeze dry the Candied Citrus Peels at -40°F for 24 to 48 hours until completely dry. Once dry, remove the candied citrus slices from the freeze dryer and let them cool to room temperature.
- **Store**: Store the freeze-dried Candied Citrus Peels in an airtight container in a cool, dry place.

Rehydrating:

- **Rehydrate**: To rehydrate, remove the desired amount from the container. Place the candied citrus slices in a bowl and cover them with hot water. The water should be just enough to cover the slices. Let the candied citrus slices soak in the hot water for about 5-10 minutes, or until they become soft and rehydrated. Drain any excess water and pat the candied citrus slices dry with a clean kitchen towel.
- **Serve**: Serve the rehydrated Candied Citrus Peels as desired, either as a sweet treat on their own or as a garnish for desserts, cocktails, or baked goods.

Chocolate-Covered Nuts

SERVINGS: 4   **PREP TIME:** 15 MIN   **COOK TIME:** 35 MIN   **FREEZE-DRY TIME:** 24-48 HRS

Ingredients:

Nuts of your choice (such as almonds, peanuts, or cashews)
Chocolate chips or melting chocolate

Optional:
Coconut oil (to thin the chocolate for dipping)
Toppings (such as sea salt, shredded coconut, or sprinkles)

Instructions:

1. Start by roasting the nuts in a preheated oven at 350°F for about 8-10 minutes, or until they are lightly golden and fragrant. Keep an eye on them to prevent burning.
2. Once roasted, remove the nuts from the oven and let them cool completely.
3. While the nuts are cooling, prepare the chocolate coating. In a microwave-safe bowl, melt the chocolate chips in the microwave in 30-second intervals, stirring between each interval until smooth. If needed, add a small amount of coconut oil or shortening to thin the chocolate for easier dipping.
4. Once the nuts are cooled, dip each nut into the melted chocolate using a fork or dipping tool, coating them completely. Allow any excess chocolate to drip off before placing them on a parchment-lined baking sheet.
5. If desired, sprinkle the chocolate-covered nuts with optional toppings like sea salt, shredded coconut, or sprinkles while the chocolate is still wet.
6. Once all the nuts are coated, place the baking sheet in the refrigerator for about 15-20 minutes, or until the chocolate has set and hardened.
7. Once the chocolate has hardened, remove the baking sheet from the refrigerator and transfer the chocolate-covered nuts to an airtight container for storage.

For Freeze-Drying:

- **Prepare**: Allow the Chocolate-Covered Nuts to cool completely and firm up on the baking sheet. Once set, carefully remove the chocolate-covered nuts from the baking sheet and transfer them to a tray or baking sheet lined with parchment paper.
- **Freeze**: Place the tray in the freezer and allow the chocolate-covered nuts to freeze completely. Once frozen, remove the chocolate-covered nuts from the freezer and transfer them to a freeze dryer.
- **Freeze Dry**: Freeze dry the Chocolate-Covered Nuts at -40°F for 24 to 48 hours until completely dry. Once dry, remove the freeze-dried Chocolate-Covered Nuts from the freeze dryer and let them cool to room temperature.
- **Store**: Store the freeze-dried Chocolate-Covered Nuts in an airtight container in a cool, dry place.

Rehydrating:

- **Rehydrate**: To rehydrate, remove the desired amount from the container. Place the chocolate-covered nuts in a bowl and cover them with hot water. The water should be just enough to cover the nuts. Let the chocolate-covered nuts soak in the hot water for about 5-10 minutes, or until they become soft and rehydrated. Drain any excess water and pat the chocolate-covered nuts dry with a clean kitchen towel.
- **Serve**: Serve the rehydrated Chocolate-Covered Nuts immediately, enjoying their crunchy texture and rich chocolate flavor.

Fruit Leather

SERVINGS: 4   **PREP TIME:** 20 MIN   **COOK TIME:** 6-8 HRS   **FREEZE-DRY TIME:** 24-48 HRS

Ingredients:

4 cups of fresh fruit (such as strawberries, apples, or mangoes), chopped

1-2 tablespoons of lemon juice (optional, for preservation and flavor)

Optional: Sweetener of choice (such as honey, maple syrup, or sugar) to taste

Instructions:

1. Preheat your oven to the lowest temperature setting (usually around 140°F).
2. Line a baking sheet with parchment paper or a silicone baking mat.
3. Place the chopped fruit in a blender or food processor and blend until smooth. If desired, you can strain the puree to remove any seeds or chunks.
4. Taste the puree and adjust the sweetness with your preferred sweetener, if needed. You can also add lemon juice for extra flavor and to help preserve the fruit leather.
5. Pour the fruit puree onto the prepared baking sheet, spreading it out evenly with a spatula to create a thin layer.
6. Place the baking sheet in the preheated oven and bake the fruit puree for 6-8 hours, or until the fruit leather is dry to the touch and no longer sticky. The exact time will depend on your oven and the thickness of the puree.
7. Once the fruit leather is dried, remove it from the oven and let it cool completely.
8. Once cooled, use kitchen scissors or a sharp knife to cut the fruit leather into strips or desired shapes.
9. Roll up the fruit leather strips and store them in an airtight container at room temperature for up to several weeks.

For Freeze-Drying:

- **Prepare**: Allow the Fruit Leather to cool completely and firm up on the baking sheet. Once set, carefully remove the fruit leather from the baking sheet and transfer it to a tray or baking sheet lined with parchment paper.
- **Freeze**: Place the tray in the freezer and allow the fruit leather to freeze completely. Once frozen, remove the fruit leather from the freezer and transfer it to a freeze dryer.
- **Freeze Dry**: Freeze dry the Fruit Leather at -40°F for 24 to 48 hours until completely dry. Once dry, remove the freeze-dried Fruit Leather from the freeze dryer and let it cool to room temperature.
- **Store**: Store the freeze-dried Fruit Leather in an airtight container in a cool, dry place.

Rehydrating:

- **Rehydrate**: To rehydrate, remove the desired amount from the container. Place the fruit leather in a bowl and cover it with hot water. The water should be just enough to cover the fruit leather. Let the fruit leather soak in the hot water for about 5-10 minutes, or until it becomes soft and pliable. Drain any excess water and pat the fruit leather dry with a clean kitchen towel.
- **Serve**: Serve the rehydrated Fruit Leather immediately, enjoying its fruity flavor and chewy texture.

Yogurt Drops

SERVINGS: 4   **PREP TIME:** 15 MIN   **COOK TIME:** 0 MIN   **FREEZE-DRY TIME:** 12-24 HRS

Ingredients:

1 cup of Greek yogurt (plain or flavored)
1-2 tablespoons of honey or maple syrup (optional, for sweetness)
Fresh fruit puree or fruit juice (optional, for flavor and color)

Instructions:

1. In a mixing bowl, combine the Greek yogurt with honey or maple syrup if using.
2. Mix well until smooth and creamy.
3. If desired, add fresh fruit puree or mashed ripe fruit to the yogurt mixture for added flavor and color.
4. Mix until well combined.

For Freeze-Drying:

- **Prepare**: Line a baking sheet with parchment paper or a silicone baking mat. Use a small spoon or a piping bag to drop small dollops of the yogurt mixture onto the prepared baking sheet, spacing them evenly apart.
- **Freeze**: Place the baking sheet in the freezer and allow the yogurt drops to freeze completely, which usually takes about 1-2 hours. Once the yogurt drops are frozen solid, remove them from the freezer and transfer them to a freeze dryer.
- **Freeze Dry**: Freeze dry the yogurt drops at -40°F for 12 to 24 hours until completely dry. Once the yogurt drops are freeze-dried and completely dry, remove them from the freeze dryer and let them cool to room temperature.
- **Store**: Store the freeze-dried yogurt drops in an airtight container in a cool, dry place away from direct sunlight.

Rehydrating:

- **Rehydrate**: To rehydrate, remove the desired amount from the container. Place the freeze-dried yogurt drops in a bowl and cover them with hot water. The water should be just enough to cover the drops. Let the yogurt drops soak in the hot water for about 5-10 minutes, or until they become soft and rehydrated. Drain any excess water and pat the yogurt drops dry with a clean kitchen towel.
- **Serve**: Enjoy the rehydrated yogurt drops as a healthy snack or as a topping for yogurt, cereal, or desserts.

Jelly Beans

SERVINGS: 4   **PREP TIME:** 3 HRS   **COOK TIME:** 15 MIN   **FREEZE-DRY TIME:** 24-48 HRS

Ingredients:

1 cup fruit juice (such as orange, apple, or grape)
1 tablespoon gelatin powder
2-3 tablespoons honey or maple syrup (adjust to taste)

Instructions:

1. In a small saucepan, pour the fruit juice and sprinkle the gelatin powder over the surface. Let it sit for a few minutes to allow the gelatin to bloom.
2. Heat the saucepan over low heat, stirring continuously until the gelatin is fully dissolved and the mixture is smooth.
3. Add honey or maple syrup to sweeten the mixture, stirring until well combined. Adjust the sweetness according to your preference.
4. Remove the saucepan from the heat and let the mixture cool slightly.
5. Once cooled, pour the mixture into candy molds or onto a baking sheet lined with parchment paper. Make sure the layer is evenly spread and not too thick.
6. Place the molds or baking sheet in the refrigerator and let the candy set for at least 2-3 hours, or until firm.
7. Once the candy is set, remove it from the molds or cut it into small jelly-like pieces if using a baking sheet.
8. If desired, you can roll the jelly beans in sugar or citric acid for extra flavor.
9. Store the jelly beans in an airtight container in the refrigerator for up to one week.

For Freeze-Drying:

- **Prepare**: Allow the Jelly beans to cool completely and firm up in the refrigerator. Once set, carefully remove the jelly beans from the molds or baking sheet and transfer them to a tray or baking sheet lined with parchment paper.
- **Freeze**: Place the tray in the freezer and allow the jelly beans to freeze completely. Once frozen, remove the jelly beans from the freezer and transfer them to a freeze dryer.
- **Freeze Dry:** Freeze dry the Jelly Beans at -40°F for 24 to 48 hours until completely dry. Once dry, remove the freeze-dried Jelly beans from the freeze dryer and let them cool to room temperature.
- **Store**: Store the freeze-dried Jelly beans in an airtight container in a cool, dry place.

Rehydrating:

- **Rehydrate**: To rehydrate, remove the desired amount from the container. Place the jelly beans in a bowl and cover them with hot water. The water should be just enough to cover the beans. Let the jelly beans soak in the hot water for about 5-10 minutes, or until they become soft and rehydrated. Drain any excess water and pat the jelly beans dry with a clean kitchen towel.
- **Serve**: Serve the rehydrated Jelly beans immediately, enjoying their fruity flavor and chewy texture.

Skittles

SERVINGS: 4   **PREP TIME:** 1 HR   **COOK TIME:** 25 MIN   **FREEZE-DRY TIME:** 24-48 HRS

Ingredients:

1 cup granulated sugar
1/4 cup light corn syrup
1/4 cup water
1/2 teaspoon flavoring extract (orange, lemon, lime, grape, strawberry, etc.)
Food coloring (assorted colors)
Granulated sugar (for coating)

Instructions:

1. In a saucepan, combine the granulated sugar, light corn syrup, and water over medium heat. Stir until the sugar is dissolved and the mixture starts to boil.
2. Insert a candy thermometer into the mixture and continue to cook, without stirring, until it reaches 300°F (hard crack stage). This should take about 10-15 minutes.
3. Remove the saucepan from heat and stir in the flavoring extract of your choice. Be careful as the mixture will be very hot.
4. Divide the candy mixture into separate bowls for each desired color. Add food coloring to each bowl and stir until well combined.
5. Using a spoon or dropper, carefully drop small amounts of the colored candy mixture onto a silicone candy mold or onto a baking sheet lined with parchment paper. Make sure to leave some space between each candy to prevent them from sticking together.
6. Let the candies cool and harden at room temperature for about 30 minutes to 1 hour.
7. Once the candies are set, remove them from the mold or use a knife to cut them into small, Skittle-like shapes if using a baking sheet.
8. Roll the candies in granulated sugar to coat them evenly.

For Freeze-Drying:

- **Prepare**: Arrange the candies on a tray or baking sheet lined with parchment paper, making sure they are not touching each other.
- **Freeze**: Place the tray in the freezer and let the candies freeze completely, preferably overnight.
- **Freeze Dry**: Freeze dry the Skittles at -40°F for 24 to 48 hours until completely dry. Once dry, remove the freeze-dried Skittles from the freeze dryer and let them cool to room temperature.
- **Store**: Store the freeze-dried candies in an airtight container in a cool, dry place.

Rehydrating:

- **Rehydrate**: To rehydrate, simply remove the Skittles from the container and eat them as they are. They should have a crunchy texture similar to Skittles. If you prefer a chewier texture, you can rehydrate the candies by soaking them in water for a few minutes. Keep in mind that they may not regain their original gummy texture but will become softer.
- **Serve**: Once rehydrated, enjoy the Skittles as a fun and tasty treat!

Starbursts

SERVINGS: 4   **PREP TIME:** 1 HR   **COOK TIME:** 25 MIN   **FREEZE-DRY TIME:** 24-48 HRS

Ingredients:

1 cup granulated sugar

1/2 cup light corn syrup

1/4 cup water

1/4 teaspoon citric acid

1/4 teaspoon flavoring extract (e.g., strawberry, lemon, orange, etc.)

Food coloring (assorted colors)

Powdered sugar (for coating)

Instructions:

1. In a saucepan, combine the granulated sugar, light corn syrup, water, and citric acid over medium heat. Stir until the sugar is dissolved and the mixture starts to boil.
2. Insert a candy thermometer into the mixture and continue to cook, without stirring, until it reaches 250°F (hard ball stage). This should take about 10-15 minutes.
3. Remove the saucepan from heat and stir in the flavoring extract of your choice. Be careful as the mixture will be very hot.
4. Divide the candy mixture into separate bowls for each desired color. Add food coloring to each bowl and stir until well combined.
5. Pour each colored candy mixture onto a separate piece of parchment paper or silicone baking mat. Use a spatula to spread the mixture into a thin, even layer.
6. Let the candy mixtures cool and harden at room temperature for about 30 minutes to 1 hour.
7. Once the candy is set, use a sharp knife or pizza cutter to cut the candy into small, Starburst-like squares or rectangles.
8. Roll each candy piece in powdered sugar to coat them evenly and prevent sticking.

For Freeze-Drying:

- **Prepare**: Arrange the Starburst-like candies on a tray or baking sheet lined with parchment paper, making sure they are not touching each other.
- **Freeze**: Place the tray in the freezer and let the candies freeze completely, preferably overnight.
- **Freeze Dry**: Freeze dry the Starbursts at -40°F for 24 to 48 hours until completely dry. Once dry, remove the freeze-dried Starbursts from the freeze dryer and let them cool to room temperature.
- **Store**: Store the freeze-dried candies in an airtight container in a cool, dry place.

Rehydrating:

- **Rehydrate**: To rehydrate, simply remove the Starbursts from the container and eat them as they are. They should have a crunchy texture similar to Starburst candies. If you prefer a chewier texture, you can try rehydrate the candies by soaking them in water for a few minutes. Keep in mind that they may not regain their original soft and chewy texture but will become softer.
- **Serve**: Once rehydrated, enjoy the Starburst-like candies as a fun and tasty treat!

Licorice

SERVINGS: 4   **PREP TIME:** 15 MIN   **COOK TIME:** 25 MIN   **FREEZE-DRY TIME:** 24-48 HRS

Ingredients:

1 cup water
1 cup granulated sugar
1 cup corn syrup
1 tablespoon anise extract
1 tablespoon black food coloring (optional)
1 cup all-purpose flour
1/4 cup powdered sugar (for coating)

Instructions:

1. In a saucepan, combine the water, granulated sugar, and corn syrup over medium heat. Stir until the sugar is dissolved and the mixture starts to boil.
2. Insert a candy thermometer into the mixture and continue to cook, without stirring, until it reaches 250°F (hard ball stage). This should take about 10-15 minutes.
3. Remove the saucepan from heat and stir in the anise extract and black food coloring, if using.
4. Gradually add the flour to the mixture, stirring continuously until well combined and the mixture forms a dough-like consistency.
5. Transfer the licorice dough to a clean surface dusted with powdered sugar. Knead the dough until smooth and pliable.
6. Roll out the dough into a thin sheet, about 1/4 inch thick.
7. Use a sharp knife or pizza cutter to cut the dough into strips or shapes resembling licorice sticks.
8. Roll each licorice strip in powdered sugar to coat them evenly and prevent sticking.

For Freeze-Drying:

- **Prepare:** Arrange the licorice strips on a tray or baking sheet lined with parchment paper, making sure they are not touching each other.
- **Freeze:** Place the tray in the freezer and let the licorice strips freeze completely, preferably overnight.
- **Freeze Dry:** Freeze dry the Licorice at -40°F for 24 to 48 hours until completely dry. Once dry, remove the freeze-dried Licorice from the freeze dryer and let them cool to room temperature.
- **Store:** Store the freeze-dried licorice strips in an airtight container in a cool, dry place.

Rehydrating:

- **Rehydrate:** To rehydrate, simply remove the Licorice from the container and eat them as they are. They should have a crunchy texture similar to licorice candy. If you prefer a softer texture, you can rehydrate the licorice strips by soaking them in warm water or milk for a few minutes. Keep in mind that they may not regain their original chewy texture but will become softer.
- **Serve:** Once rehydrated, enjoy the licorice strips as a flavorful and nostalgic treat!

M&M's

SERVINGS: 4   **PREP TIME:** 45 MIN   **COOK TIME:** 15 MIN   **FREEZE-DRY TIME:** 24-48 HRS

Ingredients:

1 cup chocolate chips (semi-sweet or milk chocolate)

1/4 cup candy-coated chocolates (like Smarties or similar candies)

1 tablespoon vegetable shortening or coconut oil

Food coloring (optional)

Instructions:

1. In a microwave-safe bowl, combine the chocolate chips and vegetable shortening or coconut oil.
2. Microwave the chocolate mixture in 30-second intervals, stirring between each interval, until the chocolate is completely melted and smooth.
3. If desired, add food coloring to the melted chocolate to achieve the desired colors for your M&M's.
4. Once the chocolate is colored (if using), gently stir in the candy-coated chocolates until they are evenly distributed throughout the chocolate mixture.
5. Line a baking sheet or tray with parchment paper. Using a small spoon or a candy mold, carefully drop small portions of the chocolate mixture onto the parchment paper, forming small, round shapes resembling M&M's.
6. Place the baking sheet in the refrigerator and let the chocolate M&M's set for at least 30 minutes, or until firm.
7. Once the M&M's are set, remove them from the refrigerator and gently peel them off the parchment paper.
8. Store the homemade M&M's in an airtight container in the refrigerator until ready to freeze-dry.

For Freeze-Drying:

- **Prepare**: Arrange the homemade M&M's on a tray or baking sheet lined with parchment paper, making sure they are not touching each other.
- **Freeze**: Place the tray in the freezer and let the M&M's freeze completely, preferably overnight.
- **Freeze Dry**: Freeze dry the M&M's at -40°F for 24 to 48 hours until completely dry. Once dry, remove the freeze-dried M&M's from the freeze dryer and let them cool to room temperature.
- **Store**: Store the freeze-dried M&M's in an airtight container in a cool, dry place.

Rehydrating:

- **Rehydrate**: To rehydrate, simply remove the M&M's from the container and eat them as they are. They should have a crunchy texture similar to regular M&M's. If you prefer a softer texture, you can rehydrate the M&M's by soaking them in warm water or milk for a few minutes. Keep in mind that they may not regain their original crunchy texture but will become softer and melty.
- **Serve**: Once rehydrated, enjoy the homemade M&M's as a delicious and colorful treat!

Peanut Brittle

SERVINGS: 4   **PREP TIME:** 15 MIN   **COOK TIME:** 25 MIN   **FREEZE-DRY TIME:** 24-48 HRS

Ingredients:

1 cup granulated sugar
1/2 cup light corn syrup
1/4 cup water
1 cup roasted peanuts (unsalted)
1 tablespoon unsalted butter
1 teaspoon vanilla extract
1 teaspoon baking soda

Instructions:

1. Line a baking sheet with parchment paper and set aside.
2. In a heavy-bottomed saucepan, combine the granulated sugar, corn syrup, and water over medium heat. Stir until the sugar is dissolved.
3. Attach a candy thermometer to the side of the saucepan and continue to cook the mixture, without stirring, until it reaches 300°F (hard crack stage). This should take about 10-15 minutes.
4. Once the mixture reaches 300°F, quickly stir in the roasted peanuts and butter. Continue cooking, stirring constantly, until the mixture turns a golden brown color and smells nutty. This should take about 2-3 minutes.
5. Remove the saucepan from heat and quickly stir in the vanilla extract and baking soda. Be careful as the mixture will bubble up.
6. Immediately pour the hot peanut brittle mixture onto the prepared baking sheet, spreading it out into an even layer with a spatula.
7. Let the peanut brittle cool completely at room temperature until hardened.
8. Once cooled and hardened, break the peanut brittle into small pieces using a knife or by hand.

For Freeze-Drying:

- **Prepare:** Arrange the peanut brittle pieces on a tray or baking sheet lined with parchment paper, making sure they are not touching each other.
- **Freeze:** Place the tray in the freezer and let the peanut brittle pieces freeze completely, preferably overnight.
- **Freeze Dry:** Freeze dry the Peanut Brittle at -40°F for 24 to 48 hours until completely dry. Once dry, remove the freeze-dried Peanut Brittle from the freeze dryer and let them cool to room temperature.
- **Store:** Store the freeze-dried peanut brittle pieces in an airtight container in a cool, dry place.

Rehydrating:

- **Rehydrate:** To rehydrate, simply remove the peanut brittle from the container and eat them as they are. They should have a crunchy texture similar to regular peanut brittle. If you prefer a softer texture, you can rehydrate the peanut brittle by soaking it in warm water or milk for a few minutes. Keep in mind that they may not regain their original crunchy texture but will become softer and melty.
- **Serve:** Once rehydrated, enjoy the peanut brittle pieces as a delicious and satisfying snack!

Candy Corn

SERVINGS: 4   **PREP TIME:** 12 HRS   **COOK TIME:** 25 MIN   **FREEZE-DRY TIME:** 24-48 HRS

Ingredients:

1 cup granulated sugar
2/3 cup light corn syrup
1/3 cup unsalted butter
1 teaspoon vanilla extract
2 1/2 cups powdered sugar
1/4 teaspoon salt
Yellow and orange food coloring

Instructions:

1. In a heavy-bottomed saucepan, combine the granulated sugar, corn syrup, and unsalted butter over medium heat. Stir until the mixture comes to a boil.
2. Once the mixture is boiling, insert a candy thermometer and continue to cook until it reaches 230°F (soft ball stage).
3. Remove the saucepan from heat and stir in the vanilla extract.
4. In a separate bowl, sift together the powdered sugar and salt.
5. Gradually add the powdered sugar mixture to the hot syrup, stirring until well combined and a dough forms.
6. Divide the dough into three equal parts. Leave one part white, color one part with yellow food coloring, and color the remaining part with orange food coloring.
7. Roll each colored dough into thin ropes, about 1/4 inch in diameter.
8. Lay the ropes side by side and press them together gently to form a long rectangle.
9. Use a sharp knife to cut the rectangle into small candy corn shapes.
10. Let the candy corn pieces cool and harden at room temperature for several hours or overnight.

For Freeze-Drying:

- **Prepare**: Arrange the candy corn pieces on a tray or baking sheet lined with parchment paper, making sure they are not touching each other.
- **Freeze**: Place the tray in the freezer and let the candy corn pieces freeze completely, preferably overnight.
- **Freeze Dry**: Freeze dry the Candy Corn at -40°F for 24 to 48 hours until completely dry. Once dry, remove the freeze-dried Candy Corn from the freeze dryer and let them cool to room temperature.
- **Store**: Store the freeze-dried candy corn pieces in an airtight container in a cool, dry place.

Rehydrating:

- **Rehydrate**: To rehydrate, simply remove the candy corn pieces from the container and eat them as they are. They should have a crunchy texture similar to regular candy corn pieces. If you prefer a softer texture, you can rehydrate the candy corn by soaking it in warm water or milk for a few minutes. Keep in mind that they may not regain their original crunchy texture but will become softer and melty.
- **Serve**: Once rehydrated, enjoy the candy corn pieces as a festive and colorful treat!

Lollipops

SERVINGS: 4   **PREP TIME:** 12 HRS   **COOK TIME:** 25 MIN   **FREEZE-DRY TIME:** 24-48 HRS

Ingredients:

1 cup granulated sugar
1/3 cup light corn syrup
1/4 cup water
1/4 teaspoon flavored extract (such as vanilla, strawberry, or lemon)
Food coloring (optional)
Lollipop sticks
Lollipop molds (optional)

Instructions:

1. Line a baking sheet with parchment paper and set aside. If using lollipop molds, lightly grease them with cooking spray.
2. In a heavy-bottomed saucepan, combine the granulated sugar, corn syrup, and water over medium heat. Stir until the sugar is dissolved.
3. Insert a candy thermometer into the saucepan and continue to cook the mixture, without stirring, until it reaches 300°F (hard crack stage). This should take about 10-15 minutes.
4. Once the mixture reaches 300°F, remove the saucepan from heat and quickly stir in the flavored extract and food coloring, if using.
5. If using lollipop molds, carefully pour the hot candy mixture into the molds, filling them to the top. If not using molds, pour small circles of the candy mixture onto the prepared baking sheet.
6. Immediately place lollipop sticks into the hot candy mixture, twisting them to coat them evenly.
7. Let the lollipops cool and harden at room temperature for several hours or until completely set.

For Freeze-Drying:

- **Prepare:** Arrange the cooled lollipops on a tray or baking sheet lined with parchment paper, making sure they are not touching each other.
- **Freeze:** Place the tray in the freezer and let the lollipops freeze completely, preferably overnight.
- **Freeze Dry:** Freeze dry the Lollipops at -40°F for 24 to 48 hours until completely dry. Once dry, remove the freeze-dried Lollipops from the freeze dryer and let them cool to room temperature.
- **Store:** Store the freeze-dried lollipops in an airtight container in a cool, dry place.

Rehydrating:

- **Rehydrate:** To rehydrate, simply remove the lollipops from the container and eat them as they are. They should have a crunchy texture similar to regular lollipops. If you prefer a softer texture, you can rehydrate the lollipops by soaking it in warm water or milk for a few minutes. Keep in mind that they may not regain their original crunchy texture but will become softer and melty.
- **Serve:** Once rehydrated, enjoy the homemade lollipops as a fun and colorful treat!

Cotton Candy

SERVINGS: 4   **PREP TIME:** 20 MIN   **COOK TIME:** 5 MIN   **FREEZE-DRY TIME:** 24-48 HRS

Ingredients:

Granulated sugar
Food coloring (optional)
Flavor extracts (optional)

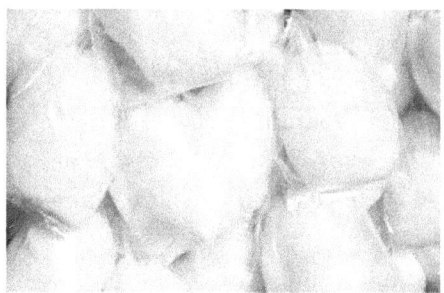

Instructions:

1. Preheat a cotton candy machine according to the manufacturer's instructions.
2. Pour granulated sugar into the cotton candy machine's spinner head.
3. Add a few drops of food coloring and flavor extract, if desired.
4. Turn on the cotton candy machine and let it spin until the sugar melts and forms thin threads of cotton candy.
5. Use a cotton candy cone or a clean fork to collect the cotton candy threads, spinning them around to form a fluffy ball.
6. Repeat the process until you have made the desired amount of cotton candy.

For Freeze-Drying:

- **Prepare**: Spread the cotton candy out on a tray or baking sheet lined with parchment paper, making sure it is spread out evenly and not clumped together.
- **Freeze**: Place the tray in the freezer and let the cotton candy freeze completely, preferably overnight.
- **Freeze Dry**: Freeze dry the cotton candy at -40°F for 24 to 48 hours until completely dry. Once dry, remove the cotton candy from the freeze dryer and let them cool to room temperature.
- **Store**: Store the cotton candy in an airtight container in a cool, dry place.

Rehydrating:

- **Rehydrate**: To rehydrate, simply remove the cotton candy from the container and eat them as they are. They should have a crunchy texture similar to regular lollipops. If you prefer a softer texture, you can try rehydrating the cotton candy by placing it in a humid environment, such as a closed container with a damp paper towel, for a few hours. Keep in mind that it may not regain its original fluffy texture but will become softer and more enjoyable to eat.
- **Serve**: Once rehydrated, enjoy the homemade cotton candy as a unique and fun treat!

Fudge

SERVINGS: 4 **PREP TIME:** 15 MIN **COOK TIME:** 15 MIN **FREEZE-DRY TIME:** 24-48 HRS

Ingredients:

3 cups granulated sugar
3/4 cup unsalted butter
2/3 cup evaporated milk
12 ounces semisweet chocolate chips
1 jar (7 ounces) marshmallow creme
1 teaspoon vanilla extract
Optional: chopped nuts or other mix-ins of your choice

Instructions:

1. Line a 9x9 inch baking pan with parchment paper, leaving some overhang on the sides for easy removal. Set aside.
2. In a large saucepan, combine the granulated sugar, unsalted butter, and evaporated milk over medium heat. Stir until the mixture comes to a boil.
3. Once boiling, continue to cook the mixture, stirring constantly, for about 5 minutes or until it reaches 234°F (soft ball stage) on a candy thermometer.
4. Remove the saucepan from heat and quickly stir in the semisweet chocolate chips until melted and smooth.
5. Stir in the marshmallow creme and vanilla extract until well combined. If using nuts or other mix-ins, fold them in at this point.
6. Pour the fudge mixture into the prepared baking pan and spread it out evenly with a spatula.
7. Let the fudge cool and set at room temperature for several hours or until completely firm.

For Freeze-Drying:

- **Prepare**: Once the fudge is completely set, cut it into small squares or desired shapes. Arrange the fudge pieces on a tray or baking sheet lined with parchment paper, making sure they are not touching each other.
- **Freeze**: Place the tray in the freezer and let the fudge freeze completely, preferably overnight.
- **Freeze Dry**: Freeze dry the fudge at -40°F for 24 to 48 hours until completely dry. Once dry, remove the freeze-dried fudge from the freeze dryer and let them cool to room temperature.
- **Store**: Store the freeze-dried fudge pieces in an airtight container in a cool, dry place.

Rehydrating:

- **Rehydrate**: To rehydrate, simply remove the fudge from the container and eat them as they are. They should have a crunchy texture similar to regular lollipops. If you prefer a softer texture, you can rehydrate the fudge by placing it in a humid environment, such as a closed container with a damp paper towel, for a few hours. Keep in mind that it may not regain its original creamy texture but will become softer and more enjoyable to eat.
- **Serve**: Once rehydrated, enjoy the homemade lollipops as a fun and colorful treat!

Peppermint Patties

SERVINGS: 4   **PREP TIME:** 12 HRS   **COOK TIME:** 25 MIN   **FREEZE-DRY TIME:** 24-48 HRS

Ingredients:

2 1/2 cups powdered sugar
1 1/2 tablespoons unsalted butter, softened
1 tablespoon light corn syrup
1/2 teaspoon peppermint extract
2 tablespoons milk
8 ounces dark chocolate, chopped

Instructions:

1. In a mixing bowl, combine the powdered sugar, softened unsalted butter, light corn syrup, peppermint extract, and milk. Mix until a smooth dough forms.
2. Shape the dough into small patties, about 1 inch in diameter, and place them on a baking sheet lined with parchment paper.
3. Place the baking sheet in the refrigerator and let the peppermint patties chill for at least 30 minutes, or until firm.
4. Meanwhile, melt the chopped dark chocolate in a heatproof bowl set over a pot of simmering water, stirring until smooth.
5. Using a fork or dipping tool, dip each chilled peppermint patty into the melted chocolate, coating it completely. Tap off any excess chocolate and place the coated patties back onto the parchment-lined baking sheet.
6. Once all the patties are coated, return the baking sheet to the refrigerator and let the chocolate set for about 30 minutes, or until firm.

For Freeze-Drying:

- **Prepare**: Arrange the chocolate-coated peppermint patties on a tray or baking sheet lined with parchment paper, making sure they are not touching each other.
- **Freeze**: Place the tray in the freezer and let the peppermint patties freeze completely, preferably overnight.
- **Freeze Dry**: Freeze dry the Peppermint Patties at -40°F for 24 to 48 hours until completely dry. Once dry, remove the Peppermint Patties from the freeze dryer and let them cool to room temperature.
- **Store**: Store the freeze-dried peppermint patties in an airtight container in a cool, dry place.

Rehydrating:

- **Rehydrate**: To rehydrate, simply remove the peppermint patties from the container and eat them as they are. They should have a crunchy texture similar to regular lollipops. If you prefer a softer texture, you can rehydrate the peppermint patties by placing it in a humid environment, such as a closed container with a damp paper towel, for a few hours. Keep in mind that they may not regain their original creamy texture but will become softer and more enjoyable to eat.
- **Serve**: Once rehydrated, enjoy the peppermint patties as a unique and delicious treat!

Chapter Eleven

Powders and Smoothies

Fruit Powder

SERVINGS: N/A **PREP TIME:** 15 MIN **COOK TIME:** 4-6 HRS **FREEZE-DRY TIME:** 24-48 HRS

Ingredients:

Fresh fruit of your choice (such as strawberries, blueberries, or mangoes)

Instructions:

1. Wash and thoroughly dry the fruit to remove any dirt or debris.
2. Slice the fruit into thin slices or small pieces, making sure they are uniform in size for even drying.
3. Arrange the fruit slices or pieces in a single layer on a baking sheet lined with parchment paper or a silicone baking mat.
4. Place the baking sheet in a preheated oven set to the lowest temperature setting (usually around 140°F).
5. Allow the fruit to dehydrate in the oven for 4 - 6 hours, rotating the baking sheet halfway through to ensure even drying.
6. Check the fruit periodically to see if it is fully dried. The fruit should be leathery and brittle when done.
7. Once dried, remove the fruit from the oven and let it cool completely.
8. Once cooled, transfer the dried fruit to a blender or food processor.
9. Blend the dried fruit until it forms a fine powder. You may need to pulse the blender or food processor several times to achieve the desired consistency.
10. Once the fruit is powdered, transfer it to an airtight container for storage.

For Freeze-Drying:

- **Prepare**: Allow the Fruit Powder to cool completely after blending. Once cooled, spread the fruit powder evenly on a tray or baking sheet lined with parchment paper.
- **Freeze**: Place the tray in the freezer and allow the fruit powder to freeze completely. Once frozen, remove the fruit powder from the freezer and transfer it to a freeze dryer.
- **Freeze Dry:** Freeze dry the Fruit Powder at -40°F for 24 to 48 hours until completely dry. Once dry, remove the freeze-dried Fruit Powder from the freeze dryer and let it cool to room temperature.
- **Store**: Store the freeze-dried Fruit Powder in an airtight container in a cool, dry place.

Rehydrating:

- **Rehydrate**: To rehydrate the freeze-dried Fruit Powder, remove the desired amount from the container. Place the fruit powder in a bowl and add a small amount of water or fruit juice. Stir the mixture until the fruit powder is fully dissolved and forms a smooth paste or liquid. Adjust the amount of water or fruit juice as needed to achieve the desired consistency.
- **Serve**: Use the rehydrated Fruit Powder immediately in recipes or as desired.

Vegetable Powder

SERVINGS: N/A   **PREP TIME:** 15 MIN   **COOK TIME:** 4-6 HRS   **FREEZE-DRY TIME:** 24-48 HRS

Ingredients:

Fresh vegetables of your choice (such as carrots, spinach, or bell peppers)

Instructions:

1. Wash and thoroughly dry the vegetables to remove any dirt or debris.
2. Chop the vegetables into small pieces, ensuring they are uniform in size for even drying.
3. Arrange the vegetable pieces in a single layer on a baking sheet lined with parchment paper or a silicone baking mat.
4. Place the baking sheet in a preheated oven set to the lowest temperature setting (usually around 140°F).
5. Allow the vegetables to dehydrate in the oven for 4 - 6 hours, rotating the baking sheet halfway through to ensure even drying.
6. Check the vegetables periodically to see if they are fully dried. They should be brittle and crisp when done.
7. Once dried, remove the vegetables from the oven and let them cool completely.
8. Once cooled, transfer the dried vegetables to a blender or food processor.
9. Blend the dried vegetables until they form a fine powder. You may need to pulse the blender or food processor several times to achieve the desired consistency.
10. Once the vegetables are powdered, transfer the vegetable powder to an airtight container for storage.

For Freeze-Drying:

- **Prepare**: Allow the Vegetable Powder to cool completely after blending. Once cooled, spread the vegetable powder evenly on a tray or baking sheet lined with parchment paper.
- **Freeze**: Place the tray in the freezer and allow the vegetable powder to freeze completely. Once frozen, remove the vegetable powder from the freezer and transfer it to a freeze dryer.
- **Freeze Dry**: Freeze dry the Vegetable Powder at -40°F for 24 to 48 hours until completely dry. Once dry, remove the freeze-dried Vegetable Powder from the freeze dryer and let it cool to room temperature.
- **Store**: Store the freeze-dried Vegetable Powder in an airtight container in a cool, dry place.

Rehydrating:

- **Rehydrate**: To rehydrate the freeze-dried Vegetable Powder, remove the desired amount from the container. Place the vegetable powder in a bowl and add hot water or vegetable broth. Stir the mixture until the vegetable powder is fully dissolved and forms a smooth paste or liquid. Adjust the amount of water or vegetable broth as needed to achieve the desired consistency.
- **Serve**: Use the rehydrated Vegetable Powder immediately in recipes or as desired.

Spice Mix Powder

SERVINGS: N/A **PREP TIME:** 15 MIN   **COOK TIME:** 0 MIN   **FREEZE-DRY TIME:** 12-24 HRS

Ingredients:

- 2 tablespoons paprika
- 1 tablespoon garlic powder
- 1 tablespoon onion powder
- 1 tablespoon ground cumin
- 1 tablespoon ground coriander
- 1 teaspoon chili powder (adjust to taste)
- 1 teaspoon dried oregano
- 1 teaspoon dried thyme
- 1 teaspoon salt (optional, adjust to taste)
- 1/2 teaspoon black pepper

Instructions:

1. In a small mixing bowl, combine all the spices and herbs.
2. Stir well until evenly mixed.
3. Taste the spice mix and adjust the seasoning if needed, adding more salt or chili powder according to your preference.

For Freeze-Drying:

- **Prepare**: Spread the spice mix evenly on a tray or baking sheet lined with parchment paper.
- **Freeze**: Place the tray in the freezer and allow the spice mix to freeze completely. Once frozen, remove the spice mix from the freezer and transfer it to a freeze dryer.
- **Freeze Dry:** Freeze dry the Spice Mix Powder at -40°F for 12 to 24 hours until completely dry. Once dry, remove the freeze-dried Spice Mix Powder from the freeze dryer and let it cool to room temperature.
- **Store**: Store the freeze-dried Spice Mix Powder in an airtight container in a cool, dry place.

Rehydrating:

- **Rehydrate**: To rehydrate the freeze-dried Spice Mix Powder, remove the desired amount from the container. Place the spice mix in a bowl and add a small amount of warm water or oil. Stir the mixture until the spice mix is fully dissolved and forms a paste or liquid. Adjust the amount of water or oil as needed to achieve the desired consistency.
- **Serve**: Use the rehydrated Spice Mix immediately in recipes or as desired.

Green Tea Powder (Matcha)

SERVINGS: N/A **PREP TIME:** 15 MIN **COOK TIME:** 2 HRS **FREEZE-DRY TIME:** 12-24 HRS

Ingredients:

High-quality green tea leaves (preferably Japanese green tea)

Instructions:

1. Start with high-quality green tea leaves. For the best matcha powder, opt for Japanese green tea leaves, specifically those meant for matcha production.
2. Spread the green tea leaves in a single layer on a baking sheet lined with parchment paper.
3. Preheat your oven to the lowest temperature setting, usually around 140°F.
4. Place the baking sheet in the oven and let the green tea leaves dry for about 1-2 hours. Keep an eye on them to prevent burning.
5. Once the leaves are dry and crisp, remove them from the oven and let them cool completely.
6. Transfer the dried green tea leaves to a clean coffee grinder or a high-powered blender.
7. Grind the dried green tea leaves into a fine powder. This may take a few minutes, depending on the power of your grinder or blender. You may need to stop and scrape down the sides of the container occasionally to ensure even grinding.
8. Once ground into a fine powder, sift the matcha powder through a fine-mesh sieve to remove any larger particles and ensure a smooth texture.

For Freeze-Drying:

- **Prepare**: Allow the Green Tea Powder to cool completely after grinding. Once cooled, spread the green tea powder evenly on a tray or baking sheet lined with parchment paper.
- **Freeze**: Place the tray in the freezer and allow the green tea powder to freeze completely. Once frozen, remove the green tea powder from the freezer and transfer it to a freeze dryer.
- **Freeze Dry**: Freeze dry the Green Tea Powder at -40°F for 12 to 24 hours until completely dry. Once dry, remove the freeze-dried Green Tea Powder from the freeze dryer and let it cool to room temperature.
- **Store**: Store the freeze-dried Green Tea Powder in an airtight container in a cool, dry place.

Rehydrating:

- **Rehydrate**: To rehydrate the freeze-dried Green Tea Powder, remove the desired amount from the container. Place the green tea powder in a bowl and add hot water (not boiling). Whisk the mixture vigorously until the green tea powder is fully dissolved and forms a frothy, smooth liquid. Adjust the amount of water as needed to achieve the desired strength of the tea.
- **Serve**: Serve the rehydrated Green Tea immediately, enjoying its vibrant color and refreshing flavor.

Coffee Powder

SERVINGS: N/A **PREP TIME:** 15 MIN **COOK TIME:** 2 HRS **FREEZE-DRY TIME:** 24-48 HRS

Ingredients:

Roasted coffee beans of your choice (such as arabica or robusta)

Instructions:

1. Start with high-quality roasted coffee beans. You can choose your preferred roast level and coffee bean variety.
2. Spread the roasted coffee beans in a single layer on a baking sheet lined with parchment paper.
3. Preheat your oven to the lowest temperature setting, usually around 140°F.
4. Place the baking sheet in the oven and let the coffee beans dry for about 1-2 hours. Keep an eye on them to prevent burning.
5. Once the beans are dry and crisp, remove them from the oven and let them cool completely.
6. Transfer the cooled roasted coffee beans to a clean coffee grinder or a high-powered blender.
7. Grind the roasted coffee beans into a fine powder. This may take a few minutes, depending on the power of your grinder or blender. You may need to stop and scrape down the sides of the container occasionally to ensure even grinding.
8. Once ground into a fine powder, sift the coffee powder through a fine-mesh sieve to remove any larger particles and ensure a smooth texture.

For Freeze-Drying:

- **Prepare**: Allow the Coffee Powder to cool completely after grinding. Once cooled, spread the coffee powder evenly on a tray or baking sheet lined with parchment paper.
- **Freeze**: Place the tray in the freezer and allow the coffee powder to freeze completely. Once frozen, remove the coffee powder from the freezer and transfer it to a freeze dryer.
- **Freeze Dry**: Freeze dry the Coffee Powder at -40°F for 24 - 48 hours until completely dry. Once dry, remove the freeze-dried Coffee Powder from the freeze dryer and let it cool to room temperature.
- **Store**: Store the freeze-dried Coffee Powder in an airtight container in a cool, dry place.

Rehydrating:

- **Rehydrate**: To rehydrate the freeze-dried Coffee Powder, remove the desired amount from the container. Place the coffee powder in a cup or mug. Add hot water to the coffee powder, using the desired amount for your preferred strength of coffee. Stir the mixture until the coffee powder is fully dissolved. Adjust the amount of water as needed to achieve the desired strength of coffee.
- **Serve**: Serve the rehydrated Coffee immediately, enjoying its rich aroma and bold flavor.

Berry Blast Smoothie

SERVINGS: N/A **PREP TIME:** 15 MIN **COOK TIME:** 0 MIN **FREEZE-DRY TIME:** 24-48 HRS

Ingredients:

1 cup mixed berries (such as strawberries, blueberries, and raspberries)
1 ripe banana
1/2 cup Greek yogurt
1/2 cup almond milk (or any milk of your choice)
1 tablespoon honey (optional, adjust to taste)
Ice cubes (optional, for a colder smoothie)

Instructions:

1. Wash the berries thoroughly and remove any stems or hulls.
2. Peel the ripe banana and cut it into chunks.
3. In a blender, combine the mixed berries, banana chunks, Greek yogurt, almond milk, and honey (if using).
4. Blend on high speed until the ingredients are smooth and well combined. If desired, add ice cubes and blend again until smooth.
5. Taste the smoothie and adjust the sweetness by adding more honey if needed.
6. Blend the smoothie to your desired consistency.

For Freeze-Drying:

- **Prepare**: Allow the Berry Blast Smoothie to return to room temperature after blending. Pour the smoothie onto a tray or baking sheet lined with parchment paper or a silicone baking mat. Spread the smoothie evenly to create a thin layer.
- **Freeze**: Place the tray in the freezer and allow the smoothie to freeze completely. Once frozen, remove the smoothie from the freezer and transfer it to a freeze dryer.
- **Freeze Dry**: Freeze dry the Berry Blast Smoothie at -40°F for 24 - 48 hours until completely dry. Once dry, remove the freeze-dried smoothie from the freeze dryer and let it cool to room temperature.
- **Store**: Store the freeze-dried smoothie in an airtight container in a cool, dry place.

Rehydrating:

- **Rehydrate**: To rehydrate the freeze-dried Berry Blast Smoothie, remove the desired amount from the container. Place the freeze-dried smoothie in a blender or food processor. Add water or milk to the blender, using the desired amount for your preferred consistency of smoothie. Blend the mixture until the freeze-dried smoothie is fully rehydrated and smooth. Adjust the amount of water or milk as needed to achieve the desired thickness of the smoothie.
- **Serve**: Pour the rehydrated Berry Blast Smoothie into glasses and serve immediately.

Tropical Delight Smoothie

SERVINGS: N/A **PREP TIME:** 15 MIN **COOK TIME:** 0 MIN **FREEZE-DRY TIME:** 24-48 HRS

Ingredients:

1 cup frozen pineapple chunks
1/2 cup frozen mango chunks
1 ripe banana
1/2 cup coconut milk
1/2 cup Greek yogurt
1 tablespoon honey or maple syrup (optional, adjust to taste)
Juice of 1/2 lime (optional, for extra tanginess)
Ice cubes (optional, for a colder smoothie)

Instructions:

1. In a blender, combine the frozen pineapple chunks, frozen mango chunks, banana, coconut milk, Greek yogurt, honey or maple syrup (if using), and lime juice (if using).
2. Blend on high speed until the ingredients are smooth and well combined. If desired, add ice cubes and blend again until smooth.
3. Taste the smoothie and adjust the sweetness by adding more honey or maple syrup if needed.
4. Blend the smoothie to your desired consistency.

For Freeze-Drying:

- **Prepare:** Allow the Tropical Delight Smoothie to return to room temperature after blending. Pour the smoothie onto a tray or baking sheet lined with parchment paper or a silicone baking mat. Spread the smoothie evenly to create a thin layer.
- **Freeze:** Place the tray in the freezer and allow the smoothie to freeze completely. Once frozen, remove the smoothie from the freezer and transfer it to a freeze dryer.
- **Freeze Dry:** Freeze dry the Tropical Delight Smoothie at -40°F for 24 - 48 hours until completely dry. Once dry, remove the freeze-dried smoothie from the freeze dryer and let it cool to room temperature.
- **Store:** Store the freeze-dried smoothie in an airtight container in a cool, dry place

Rehydrating:

- **Rehydrate:** To rehydrate the freeze-dried Tropical Delight Smoothie, remove the desired amount from the container. Place the freeze-dried smoothie in a blender or food processor. Add water or coconut water to the blender, using the desired amount for your preferred consistency of smoothie. Blend the mixture until the freeze-dried smoothie is fully rehydrated and smooth. Adjust the amount of water or coconut water as needed to achieve the desired thickness of the smoothie.
- **Serve:** Pour the rehydrated Tropical Delight Smoothie into glasses and serve immediately.

Green Goddess Smoothie

SERVINGS: N/A   **PREP TIME:** 15 MIN   **COOK TIME:** 0 MIN   **FREEZE-DRY TIME:** 24-48 HRS

Ingredients:

1 ripe banana
1 cup fresh spinach leaves
1/2 cup chopped cucumber
1/2 cup chopped pineapple
1/2 cup chopped mango
1/2 cup coconut water or almond milk
1 tablespoon chia seeds (optional)
Juice of 1/2 lime (optional, for extra tanginess)
Ice cubes (optional, for a colder smoothie)

Instructions:

1. In a blender, combine the ripe banana, fresh spinach leaves, chopped cucumber, chopped pineapple, chopped mango, coconut water or almond milk, chia seeds (if using), and lime juice (if using).
2. Blend on high speed until the ingredients are smooth and well combined. If desired, add ice cubes and blend again until smooth.
3. Taste the smoothie and adjust the sweetness or tanginess by adding more fruit or lime juice if needed.
4. Blend the smoothie to your desired consistency.

For Freeze-Drying:

- **Prepare**: Allow the Green Goddess Smoothie to return to room temperature after blending. Pour the smoothie onto a tray or baking sheet lined with parchment paper or a silicone baking mat. Spread the smoothie evenly to create a thin layer.
- **Freeze**: Place the tray in the freezer and allow the smoothie to freeze completely. Once frozen, remove the smoothie from the freezer and transfer it to a freeze dryer.
- **Freeze Dry**: Freeze dry the Green Goddess Smoothie at -40°F for 24 - 48 hours until completely dry. Once dry, remove the freeze-dried smoothie from the freeze dryer and let it cool to room temperature.
- **Store**: Store the freeze-dried smoothie in an airtight container in a cool, dry place

Rehydrating:

- **Rehydrate**: To rehydrate the freeze-dried Green Goddess Smoothie, remove the desired amount from the container. Place the freeze-dried smoothie in a blender or food processor. Add water or coconut water to the blender, using the desired amount for your preferred consistency of smoothie. Blend the mixture until the freeze-dried smoothie is fully rehydrated and smooth. Adjust the amount of water or coconut water as needed to achieve the desired thickness of the smoothie.
- **Serve**: Pour the rehydrated Green Goddess Smoothie into glasses and serve immediately.

Peanut Butter Banana Smoothie

SERVINGS: N/A   **PREP TIME:** 15 MIN   **COOK TIME:** 0 MIN   **FREEZE-DRY TIME:** 24-48 HRS

Ingredients:

1 ripe banana
2 tablespoons peanut butter (smooth or crunchy)
1 cup milk (dairy or plant-based)
1/2 cup Greek yogurt
1 tablespoon honey or maple syrup (optional, adjust to taste)
Ice cubes (optional, for a colder smoothie)

Optional add-ins: a handful of spinach leaves, a tablespoon of chia seeds, a scoop of protein powder

Instructions:

1. Peel the ripe banana and slice it into chunks.
2. In a blender, combine the banana chunks, peanut butter, milk, Greek yogurt, and honey or maple syrup (if using).
3. Blend on high speed until the ingredients are smooth and well combined. If desired, add ice cubes and blend again until smooth.
4. Taste the smoothie and adjust the sweetness by adding more honey or maple syrup if needed.
5. Blend the smoothie to your desired consistency.

For Freeze-Drying:

- **Prepare:** Allow the Peanut Butter Banana Smoothie to return to room temperature after blending. Pour the smoothie onto a tray or baking sheet lined with parchment paper or a silicone baking mat. Spread the smoothie evenly to create a thin layer.
- **Freeze:** Place the tray in the freezer and allow the smoothie to freeze completely. Once frozen, remove the smoothie from the freezer and transfer it to a freeze dryer.
- **Freeze Dry:** Freeze dry the Peanut Butter Banana Smoothie at -40°F for 24 - 48 hours until completely dry. Once dry, remove the freeze-dried smoothie from the freeze dryer and let it cool to room temperature.
- **Store:** Store the freeze-dried smoothie in an airtight container in a cool, dry place

Rehydrating:

- **Rehydrate:** To rehydrate the freeze-dried Peanut Butter Banana Smoothie, remove the desired amount from the container. Place the freeze-dried smoothie in a blender or food processor. Add milk or water to the blender, using the desired amount for your preferred consistency of smoothie. Blend the mixture until the freeze-dried smoothie is fully rehydrated and smooth. Adjust the amount of liquid as needed to achieve the desired thickness of the smoothie.
- **Serve:** Pour the rehydrated Peanut Butter Banana Smoothie into glasses and serve immediately.

Chocolate Mocha Smoothie

SERVINGS: N/A   **PREP TIME:** 15 MIN   **COOK TIME:** 0 MIN   **FREEZE-DRY TIME:** 24-48 HRS

Ingredients:

1 ripe banana
1 cup brewed coffee, cooled
1/2 cup milk (dairy or plant-based)
2 tablespoons unsweetened cocoa powder
1 tablespoon honey or maple syrup (optional, adjust to taste)
1/2 teaspoon vanilla extract
Ice cubes (optional, for a colder smoothie)

Optional add-ins: a handful of spinach leaves, a scoop of chocolate protein powder

Instructions:

1. Peel the ripe banana and slice it into chunks.
2. In a blender, combine the banana chunks, brewed coffee, milk, cocoa powder, honey or maple syrup (if using), and vanilla extract.
3. Blend on high speed until the ingredients are smooth and well combined. If desired, add ice cubes and blend again until smooth.
4. Taste the smoothie and adjust the sweetness by adding more honey or maple syrup if needed.
5. Blend the smoothie to your desired consistency.

For Freeze-Drying:

- **Prepare:** Allow the Chocolate Mocha Smoothie to return to room temperature after blending. Pour the smoothie onto a tray or baking sheet lined with parchment paper or a silicone baking mat. Spread the smoothie evenly to create a thin layer.
- **Freeze:** Place the tray in the freezer and allow the smoothie to freeze completely. Once frozen, remove the smoothie from the freezer and transfer it to a freeze dryer.
- **Freeze Dry:** Freeze dry the Chocolate Mocha Smoothie at -40°F for 24 - 48 hours until completely dry. Once dry, remove the freeze-dried smoothie from the freeze dryer and let it cool to room temperature.
- **Store:** Store the freeze-dried smoothie in an airtight container in a cool, dry place

Rehydrating:

- **Rehydrate:** To rehydrate the freeze-dried Chocolate Mocha Smoothie, remove the desired amount from the container. Place the freeze-dried smoothie in a blender or food processor. Add brewed coffee or milk to the blender, using the desired amount for your preferred consistency of smoothie. Blend the mixture until the freeze-dried smoothie is fully rehydrated and smooth. Adjust the amount of liquid as needed to achieve the desired thickness of the smoothie.
- **Serve:** Pour the rehydrated Chocolate Mocha Smoothie into glasses and serve immediately.

Measurements & Conversions

Tablespoon	Teaspoon	Cup	Ounces
1 tbsp	3 tsp	1/16 cup	½ oz
3 tbsp	9 tsp	⅛ cup	1 oz
4 tbsp	12 tsp	¼ cup	2 oz
5.5 tbsp	16.5 tsp	⅓ cup	2.5 oz
6 tbsp	18 tsp	⅜ cup	3 oz
8 tbsp	24 tsp	½ cup	4 oz
11 tbsp	33 tsp	⅔ cup	5 oz
12 tbsp	36 tsp	¾ cup	6 oz
16 tbsp	48 tsp	1 cup	8 oz
32 tbsp	96 tsp	2 cup	16 oz
64 tbsp	192 tsp	4 cup	32 oz
80 tbsp	240 tsp	5 cup	40 oz
96 tbsp	288 tsp	6 cup	48 oz
128 tbsp	284 tsp	8 cup	64 oz

FREE DOWNLOAD

THE ULTIMATE
FREEZE DRYING BOOK

INSIDE YOU'LL FIND:
BATCH LOGS, CONVERSATION CHARTS, CANDY LOGS, REHYDRATION LOGS, MAINTENANCE LOGS, SUPPLY LOGS & MUCH MORE

SCAN ME

Conclusion

As we conclude this journey through the fascinating world of freeze-drying, we find ourselves filled with a profound sense of accomplishment and wonder. Together, we've delved into the intricacies of this preservation technique, unlocking its potential to transform everyday ingredients into culinary delights that defy time and space. From fruits to meats, vegetables to desserts, the possibilities are as endless as our imagination allows.

Throughout this cookbook, we have strived to impart not only the techniques and recipes but also a deep appreciation for the artistry and science behind freeze-drying. We've discovered that freeze-drying isn't just about preserving food; it's about preserving flavors, textures, and memories. It's about capturing the essence of each ingredient in its purest form, allowing us to savor its freshness long after it's been harvested or prepared.

As we reflect on our culinary journey, we cannot help but marvel at the versatility of freeze-dried ingredients. Whether we're creating gourmet meals for special occasions or packing snacks for our outdoor adventures, freeze-dried foods have become indispensable in our kitchens. They offer convenience without compromise, allowing us to enjoy wholesome, flavorful meals wherever and whenever we please.

But freeze-drying is more than just a convenient way to preserve food; it's also a sustainable solution to reducing food waste. By freeze-drying surplus produce or leftovers, we can extend their shelf life and minimize the amount of food that ends up in landfills. In a world where food security and environmental sustainability are increasingly important, freeze-drying emerges as a powerful tool in our culinary arsenal.

Moreover, freeze-drying empowers us to explore new culinary horizons and push the boundaries of our creativity. With freeze-dried ingredients at our fingertips, we can experiment with flavors and textures in ways we never thought possible. We can reimagine classic dishes, reinvent old favorites, and invent entirely new culinary creations that showcase the full potential of freeze-dried ingredients.

In our journey together, we've encountered challenges and setbacks, but we've also experienced moments of triumph and discovery. We've learned to navigate the intricacies of freeze-drying equipment, troubleshoot common issues, and adapt recipes to suit our tastes and preferences. And through it all, we've grown not just as cooks but as innovators, pioneers, and stewards of culinary tradition.

As we bid farewell to this cookbook, we do so with a sense of gratitude for the opportunity to embark on this culinary adventure together. We extend our heartfelt thanks to the pioneers and experts who have shared their knowledge and expertise, as well as to our fellow home cooks who have inspired us with their creativity and ingenuity. And we invite you, dear reader, to continue exploring the possibilities of freeze-drying in your own kitchen, armed with the skills, knowledge, and confidence you've gained along the way.

In closing, let's remember that freeze-drying is not just a technique; it's a journey—a journey of exploration, experimentation, and endless discovery. So, let us continue to push the boundaries, challenge the norms, and unlock the full potential of freeze-drying in all its forms. Together, we can create a future where delicious, nutritious food is not just preserved but celebrated, cherished, and enjoyed to the fullest. If you enjoyed this book and all the recipes, please leave us your honest review on Amazon. It will only take 2 minutes, but it will help so many people find this book when they need it most. Thank you for joining us on this incredible journey. Until we meet again in the kitchen, happy freeze-drying!

Publisher

HarvestGuard Publications is a leading brand specializing in comprehensive and accessible resources for freeze-drying novices. Our mission is to demystify the art and science of freeze-drying, making it approachable and practical for everyone—from homemakers wanting to preserve food to hobbyists interested in freeze-drying flowers or other items.

At HarvestGuard Publications, we recognize the diverse applications and potentials of freeze-drying technology. That's why our books range from introductory guides to more specialized texts that dive deep into specific freeze-drying techniques and their uses in various industries like food preservation, pharmaceuticals, and even space travel.

Our educational materials rely on a foundation of evidence-based research and hands-on experience in the field of freeze-drying. We focus on simplifying complex concepts and methodologies, ensuring that our readers can easily comprehend and apply the information. Our guides prioritize safety and efficiency, offering step-by-step instructions, tips, and tricks that have been vetted by experts in the field.

By adopting a straightforward and user-friendly approach, HarvestGuard Publications aims to make freeze-drying not just a highly specialized technique but a practical skill that can be mastered and enjoyed by all. We believe that with the right information and guidance, anyone can benefit from this amazing preservation method, making it a valuable addition to households and businesses alike.

www.ingramcontent.com/pod-product-compliance
Lightning Source LLC
Chambersburg PA
CBHW082208070526
44585CB00020B/2332